CAPS / ONE SIZE FITS ALL

CAPS / ONE SIZE FITS ALL

STEVEN BRYDEN

PRESTEL
MUNICH • LONDON • NEW YORK

Cap street style in New York.

CONTENTS

INTRODUCTION
STEVEN BRYDEN

My relationship with caps started at an early age. My father dragged me to the barbershop for my monthly haircut, telling me that my Afro was getting a tidy-up. This wasn't the case. Instead, he told the barber: 'Take it all off.'

I stepped out of the barber's chair with an unexpectedly shiny ball-shaped head. Feeling self-conscious about my bare scalp, I took my dad's cap off his head and put it on mine. The hat was a bright red Marlboro promotional cap that my dad had got from a friend, and he let me keep it. I wore it whenever and wherever possible. I got strange looks every time I wore it – in retrospect, it was probably the branding that people were staring at – but having the cap made me feel special. I didn't see anybody else wearing it. I felt rebellious. Plus I thought it looked cool. I wore that cap so much that the sun turned it pink.

My obsession with caps continued from there. After that first cap, my gateway drug, I wore a few mesh trucker-style hats, as well as some with BMX manufacturers' logos. My obsession really escalated because of my interest in music. In the late 1980s, hip-hop was on the rise. Vinyl album artwork taught me which caps artists were wearing and which American sports teams were popular. Then MTV beamed that information into living rooms around the world, and I was sold.

At the time there were only a handful of stores in London that sold American sports team baseball caps: Slick Willies in Kensington, Passenger in Soho and MASH on Oxford Street. Until I went to the States, these places were my Mecca. They were expensive, but I was a regular customer. Finally, in 1989, I took my first flight to the homeland of baseball. The rest is history.

Since then, I haven't stopped wearing caps. I feel naked if I leave home without one on. And I'm not the only one: the number of people who wear baseball caps is at an all-time high. There are many of us who throw them on each morning, unaware of how much this humble design has changed fashion on global scale.

Caps are associated with victory even beyond baseball. When a Formula One driver wins a race, or a basketball player wins a playoff, the first thing he or she does is put their cap on. Caps also have a significance beyond their function as part of a working wardrobe or uniform: style.

A decade ago, my peers and I were fixated on matching our caps to our shoes and shirts. This phase is now over, but I still make a conscious effort to ensure that the cap I'm wearing looks right with my attire. Over the years, I've accumulated various styles, from military hats to wacky promotional painter's caps. They all mean something to me; they each play a part in my life. The Internet has changed the spirit of cap hunting, making it easier to obtain what was once unreachable, but the fun of it hasn't disappeared. In fact, it's got loads better.

The cap's place as a global cultural icon is now cemented. Though trends fade, each new subculture adopts this style of headwear as their own; each wearer's choice of cap broadcasts whatever they want to say about themselves. For this reason, the cap is here to stay – and will remain forever on my head.

Opposite: Author Steven Bryden wearing his first cap as a child.

THE CAP: A HISTORY
GARY WARNETT

Loved, hated, collected and respected, it's curious to think that something as basic as a baseball cap could have snowballed into such a huge phenomenon over its 150+ years of existence, spawning numerous variants and becoming ever richer in its social connotations. What's projected onto it by society is arguably more significant than what has been sewn and printed on its crown.

The peaked hat took many forms before it ever offered a solution to the problem of how to protect your head on game day. The flat cap evolved from a 14th-century design to an item of apparel prescribed by law in Great Britain, where between 1571 and 1597, a daily fine was imposed upon any non-noble male person over the age of 6 who failed to wear a woollen hat on Sundays or holidays. From there, it also became the preferred golfing headgear of the upper classes. When it was taken to America by British and Irish immigrants at the beginning of the 19th century, the cap's everyman status went international.

In the early 1800s, the bonnet developed a peak to protect women from the sun. A different kind of peaked hat became a military staple among higher-ranking Russian and Prussian army officers (in a design that had started off without a peak) around the same time. By the 1850s, the peaked cap had superseded more elaborate forms of headwear for US troops, since it was a functional item for comfortable combat in warmer conditions.

Just as America was embracing military wear, a baseball craze also erupted, and a variety of headwear – including straw hats – was worn by players and fans. Historical accounts reveal that flat-topped peaked designs and even a bowler-style effort were tried on for size, but Brooklyn's Excelsiors get credit for introducing the original round-top baseball cap in 1860. From there, regional variants became a staple of the sport. By the early 1900s, there was already a wealth of options: a flat-topped Chicago style, a deep-crowned Philadelphia

Opposite: A young David Koch, former CEO of New Era (and grandson of the company's founder), featured in a 1950s catalogue wearing a short-billed cap.

The Excelsiors of Brooklyn, 1860.

CAPS: ONE SIZE FITS ALL

style, the New York style (very much the archetype for contemporary baseball caps), the aforementioned Brooklyn style, the round Boston style and the college style – which was, like the Chicago variation, flat like a painter's cap, but less detailed. In each version, bill sizes and shapes went through multiple variants too. Horse hair was a key material in these creations, but even at this point in time, a ventilated crown, visor stitching and a perspiration-proof sweatband were standard in the majority of designs.

The traditional peaked cap once held the position that the baseball cap would ultimately take: being the cap of the everyman. Manchester's feared and detested teen gangs, whose members were known as 'scuttlers', wore the peaked cap as part of their uniform as the 19th century drew to a close.

In the 20th century, the baseball cap would spread to every class and subculture, going far beyond the baseball pitch. Fitted or fastened, its affordability made it a democratic form of headwear, just like the caps of previous centuries. The cap became synonymous with sports beyond baseball, as well as with music and other modes of entertainment. Between 1860 and the present day, the baseball cap has become all things to all people.

The cap is still standard issue in some military fields, and it's worn by lawbreakers and lawmakers alike. Though it was once a legal obligation to wear one, it can now be banned in an establishment or a public place because of its associations with anonymity and troublemaking. It denotes tribal membership, identifying the wearer as a team member or supporter, but can also be worn as an act of individuality or rebellion. The cap can hide and it can highlight, and though its beginnings were simple and functional, its meanings today are almost infinite.

Gary Warnett is a freelance journalist, copywriter and brand consultant. He is editor and content manager of Crooked Tongues, the online store for men's sneakers. He has written for magazines including Complex, Sneaker Freaker, i-D, POP, L'Uomo Vogue, Men's Health *and* Time Out *and is a consultant for Nike UK.*

ANATOMY OF A CAP

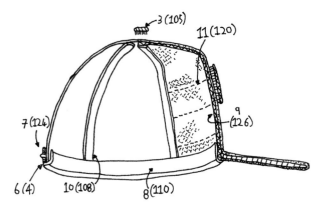

Caps are produced in all shapes and sizes, but all are made to be either fitted or adjustable. Fitted caps, which can't be adjusted to the individual wearer, are used in Major League Baseball (MLB). Most military-style caps are fitted too. Adjustable caps have closures at the rear that come in several different styles, from plastic snaps to leather straps with metal buckles and Velcro. Other methods of fitting include pull-cords and elasticated rears.

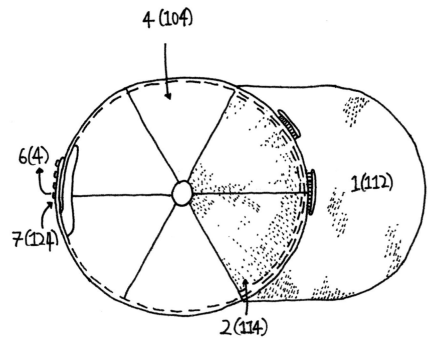

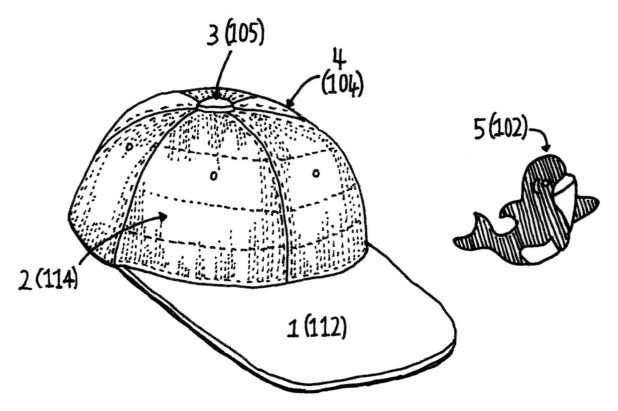

3 (105)
4 (104)
5 (102)
2 (114)
1 (112)

DRAWING KEY

1   Brim: shades the wearer from sunlight.
2   Crown: the front of the hat that touches the forehead.
3   Button: the round circle at the top of the hat; it holds the panels together.
4   Panels: parts of the cap that form its shape; they sometimes feature eyelets for ventilation.
5   The lucky dolphin emblem.
6/7 Closure: most caps have a closure at the rear, unless they are fitted.
8   Sweatband: a customary part of all caps; they catch sweat.
9   Buckram: the liner inside the front of a cap that provides structure and form.
10 Tape: covers the turned edges in the interior of the cap and adds comfort and support to the panels.
11 Logo: a mark or representation of a brand, company or statement.

Drawings based on Richard C. Soergel and S.T. Yang's 1996 patent for a baseball cap configured to permit different logos to be interchangeably positioned on the front (U.S. Patent 5,509,144).

CAR CAPS

NEW NOVELTY CAP FOR BOYS WITH CAR NAME AND EMBLEM

CAP COLORS:
Red, Royal, Kelly

Available with following car emblems: Ford, Cadillac, Oldsmobile, Mercury, Buick, Chevrolet, Pontiac, Plymouth, Chrysler

RAILROAD TRAVEL CAPS

With emblems of leading railroads
Cap colors: Red, Royal, Kelly.

AIRLINE TRAVEL CAPS

With emblems of leading airlines
Cap colors: Red, Royal, Kelly.

American Needle & Novelty Co.

2846 W. NORTH AVENUE
CHICAGO 47, ILLINOIS

A vintage American Needle advertisement.

MAJOR PLAYERS

The brands in this section kickstarted the whole of cap culture. They originally created their caps to be a functional part of uniforms, and some of them still are. However, most MLB matches are now played at night, so there's really no reason for the teams to wear caps; the fact that they do proves that caps have transcended their previous role as equipment and become a tradition. The brands in this section make caps for people who are passionate about them – the construction, colour, fit and, of course, the team, company or logo they represent.

Caps are now a global phenomenon, and are sold by the millions in malls, markets and via the Internet. Over the years, cap styles have transformed, but the basic construction – a crown with a peak – has been a constant. This simple shape is a blank canvas, and these godfather brands have now gone beyond their original mission of using it to produce hats for sports teams and begun to pursue other sources of revenue.

Ehrhardt Koch (centre), with other members of the New Era staff, 1930s.

NEW ERA CAP CO., INC.

Co-founder Ehrhardt Koch, back right, and other workers at the New Era factory, Buffalo, 1920s.

In 1920, the German immigrant Ehrhardt Koch borrowed $1,000 from his sister Rose in order to set up the E. Koch Cap Co. in the city of Buffalo, New York. In 1922, the name of the company was officially changed to the New Era Cap Co., and business took off: soon New Era was making 60,000 caps per year. At first the company produced casual and uniform caps, including newsboy-type wool hats, rather than the sporting caps it's known for today. But in the late 1920s and early 1930s, baseball enjoyed a huge rise in popularity in America, and the company saw an opportunity to capitalize on this by making caps for baseball teams.

In 1934, New Era's caps were worn on the field by a professional baseball team for the first time: the Cleveland Indians. The company also supplied local college and Minor League teams, in addition to selling plain caps onto which customers could sew their own labels.

New Era developed its first adjustable cap in the late 1940s, and in the 1950s, when Ehrhardt's son Harold joined the company, new innovations followed. Harold modernized the fitted pro cap and renamed it the 59FIFTY or 'Brooklyn-style' cap. He also introduced the top stitch (a decorative stitch around the base) and the cotton sweatband, both of which are now found in all baseball caps around the world.

By 1974, 20 of the 24 professional baseball teams in America were supplied with caps by New Era. In 1978, the company placed an advertisement in national sports publication *The Sporting News*, offering to sell pro-style fitted baseball caps to fans for $12.99. The demand was huge, and encouraged the company to sell directly to the public.

In 1986, the first ever version of the Diamond Collection 59FIFTY, which was now an official on-field product, began to be sold in stores. Fans could now wear the same caps that were worn by professional players. And in 1991, the MLB logo was added to the back of every cap in the Authentic Collection. New Era signed a deal to be the official on-field cap of every MLB team in 1993.

New York filmmaker Spike Lee asked the company to produce a red Yankees fitted cap for him in 1996. During the World Series that year, Lee appeared on TV in the notorious cap, exposing it to a huge audience of viewers across the USA. Demand for New Era caps shot up.

Nowadays New Era are known for their collaborations with many well-known and up-and-coming fashion labels, as well as with brands outside the worlds of fashion and sport, such as Marvel and DC Comics.

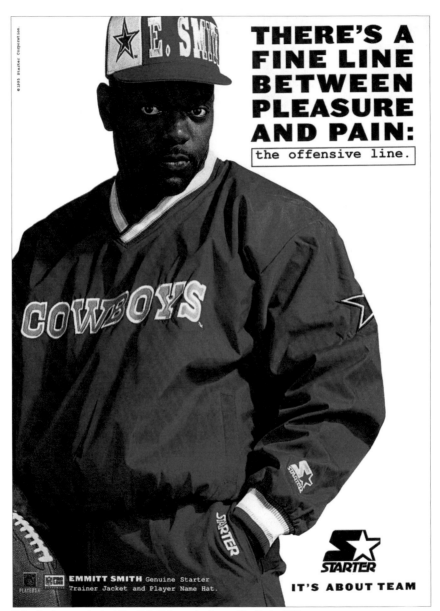

Dallas Cowboys running back Emmitt Smith in an advertisement for Starter, 1995.

STARTER

In 1971, David Beckerman, a former basketball player for Southern Connecticut State University, founded Starter in the town of New Haven. His aim was to manufacture uniforms for high school sports teams. In 1976, the company signed non-exclusive licencing agreements with several professional sports leagues, who agreed that they could manufacture and sell reproductions of professional sports uniforms. For this they paid the leagues a royalty of between 8 and 10 per cent.

By the mid-1980s, Starter was working in partnerships with major professional leagues in basketball, football, baseball and hockey, as well as 150 colleges and universities across America. The company's first retail product was a line of jackets emblazoned with the insignias of MLB teams. The 1990s saw Starter expand into over 25 countries around the world. It was one of the most

recognized brands in sports apparel at that time, and even became the official sponsor of the Atlanta Olympic Games in 1996. Starter's innovation was to place its embroidered logo on the backs of baseball caps and the sleeves of jackets. It was fashionable in the 1990s to wear baseball caps backwards, so the Starter 'S' and star logo would be visible before you could even see the branding of the team itself. In the late 1990s, Starter also began to work with leading athletes and personalities from hip-hop, film and TV.

Starter was re-launched in 2008 with a new spokesperson: Tony Romo, the starting quarterback for the Dallas Cowboys. A licence agreement with Refuel Brand Distribution Ltd in 2010 led to the founding of Starter Black Label in Europe, which built on the brand's crossover success of the 1990s.

The Mitchell & Ness store on Arch Street, Philadelphia, which opened in 1904.

CAPS: ONE SIZE FITS ALL

MITCHELL & NESS NOSTALGIA CO.

Established in 1904 as a sporting goods store in Philadelphia by tennis and wrestling champion Frank P. Mitchell and golfer Charles M. Ness, Mitchell & Ness Sporting Goods was recruited to be official on-field outfitters to the Philadelphia Eagles in 1933. The caps and apparel worn by the players soon became fashionable off the field too. As the company's status began to grow, so did the fashion industry's interest in it, as Mitchell & Ness established its position in the street- and sportswear markets.

Mitchell & Ness's signature snapbacks are made with high-end materials in a now-classic, unique shape. They can be worn by both men and women. The company benefits from the current popularity of the vintage aesthetic, since its products have a strong emphasis on sporting history and nostagia. It aims to create premium products by focusing on detail, materials and construction. In Europe Mitchell & Ness manufactures clothing, hats and accessories under licence for the National Basketball Association, the National Collegiate Athletic Association and the National Hockey League.

Announcement in the Philadelphia Eagles programme, 1940.

THE IMPROVED
HOME RUN=BASE BALL CAP

New - Shape — Non-Breakable Visor — New Emblem

A Better Cap - throughout, but it still is

A 25c RETAILER

Write for

Samples

and Prices

—

Do it Now

No. 335

Made in
Following Colors

—

NAVY BLUE

DARK RED

GREY (Red Peak)

GREY (Blue Peak)

—

Description:—Made of excellent quality suede cloth; non-breakable waterpoof visor—taped seams imitation leather sweat; home run emblem. A superior cap in every particular. Furnished in the following colors—navy, dark red, and gray. Assorted sizes to the dozen. Packed solid colors.

MANUFACTURED BY

AMERICAN NEEDLE & NOVELTY CO.

1908-10 W. NORTH AVE., CHICAGO, ILL.

MANUFACTURERS OF HEADWEAR SPECIALTIES

A vintage American Needle advertisement.

AMERICAN NEEDLE

American Needle factory, 1929.

American Needle was founded on the north side of Chicago in 1918 as the American Needle and Novelty Co., a company that imported sewing needles and made visors for bank tellers. After quickly moving into the manufacture of caps and hats, and enjoying some success with these, the company decided to approach Philip 'P.K.' Wrigley, chewing-gum manufacturer and MLB executive, with an idea: they wanted to sell Chicago Cubs caps, just like the ones the team wore, to fans at the famous Wrigley Field baseball ground. Wrigley agreed, though he expressed some doubts: 'Who would want to buy the hats the players are wearing?', he asked.

Luckily for American Needle, Wrigley's pessimism was unfounded, and this early instance of sports merchandising was a huge success. The first production run of the Cubs hats the company made sold out in a single day, and a second run faster still.

The company began to make apparel for other MLB teams and, later, for Minor League teams as well. From the late 1970s to 2000, they would also produce sports apparel under licence to the National Football League (NFL).

Today, American Needle supplies licenced headwear in the fields of baseball, hockey, tennis and golf, as well as offering a bespoke cap-making service. It prides itself on craftsmanship, holding over 30 patents on design and manufacturing innovations, while remaining always aware of its history.

Ebbets Field Flannels catalogue cover, 1992.

CAPS: ONE SIZE FITS ALL

EBBETS FIELD FLANNELS

Ebbets Field has been making flannel caps for over 20 years. Founder Jerry Cohen grew up fascinated with sports insignia and uniforms, and baseball cards were his points of reference. Cohen observed minute changes in uniform styles when most people's attention was on the players themselves.

In 1987, Cohen was trying to locate a vintage flannel baseball jersey to wear onstage with his rock 'n' roll band. Not satisfied with what was on offer, he became determined to create his own. He managed to obtain some old wool baseball flannel and had a few shirts made. The feedback was so positive that he decided to go into manufacturing flannels for other people, and Ebbets Field Flannels was officially born.

Ebbets decided to focus on non-Major League teams, including the Negro Leagues and the pre-1958 Pacific Coast League. This direction gave the company a unique twist in comparison to the others around at the time, and brought lesser-known facets of baseball history to a larger audience. The company's first cap was made in 1989 and they still use original manufacturing techniques. Their caps have been featured in movies and on TV shows, and have appeared on Major League diamonds in numerous 'Turn Back the Clock' games. One of their proudest moments was on the closing day of the old Yankee Stadium, when Ebbets Field uniforms adorned Yankee legends like Yogi Berra and Whitey Ford.

In more recent times, Ebbets Field has produced caps for a variety of brands outside the world of baseball. They are committed to bringing superior craftsmanship and knowledge to assist these brands in producing their own caps. However, their mission has always been to make caps faithful to the originals, as worn by the players from 1900 through to 1970. They are true to the original fabrics and crown structure, the way the letters are cut and sewn and smaller details, like under-visors.

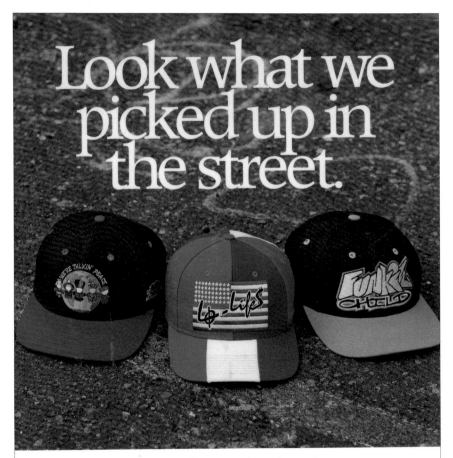

Look what we picked up in the street.

How do you pick up the country's leading hip hop cap line?

For us, we went to the source.

For the first time ever, we asked high school students to design hip hop caps. And they jumped at the chance.

Check the winners in our first Street Noyz™ Student Design Competition. With our new competition breaking in magazines this fall, there are more designs

and more winners on the way.

And even more distance between the Noyz and the also-rans.

Pick up Street Noyz at a store near you. They are the first and only caps designed in the streets.

If it's a genuine Street Noyz cap, you'll know it on the back.

The Street Noyz Student Design Competition

Street Noyz
by Signatures

Street Noyz is a registered trademark of Signatures Sportswear

In the 1990s, the label's Street Noyz line featured designs by high-school students.

SPORTS SPECIALTIES CORPORATION

NBA top first-round draft picks in New York, 1986. L to R: Kenny 'Sky' Walker, Chuck Person, Brad Daugherty, Len Bias and Chris Washburn.

The Sports Specialties Corporation was originally founded in 1928 by David Warsaw. Warsaw's sons, James and Robert, joined the family business in 1969, and together they made Sports Specialties into one of the world's top licenced sports headwear companies.

Based in Irvine, California, Sports Specialties became the first official licencee of the NFL in 1963. It was also the first company to be named as an official supplier of headwear for special sporting events, such as the NBA Finals and Super Bowl. It also produced apparel under licence for the NFL ProLine and MLB in 1984, competing against New Era for the on-field cap market.

Sports Specialties' caps were used by various MLB teams throughout the 1980s, and by the 1990s they were a strong competitor of New Era: more than half of all MLB teams used their caps for at least one season.

In 1994, New Era obtained an exclusive licencing contract for all MLB teams. Unwilling to stop producing, Sports Specialties continued to make their on-field MLB caps, but sold them as 'generic' rather than official versions. In the mid-1990s, the company was sold to Nike. It finally left the MLB cap market at the end of the 1990s.

Clockwise from top left: Seattle Supersonics, Official Stay, Stussy Cord, Boston Celtics.

CAP DATA

Here is a cross-section of noteworthy cap designs from both the past and the present. While some are iconic, others were selected for their desirability, uniqueness or status in cap culture. Several of these examples have been given nicknames by the cap community and certain styles have started trends.

From sportswear labels to streetwear brands, understated designs to offbeat styles, and instantly recognizable classics to limited-edition exclusives, the selection shows that the cap is a deceptively simple template from which a myriad of design permutations are possible. While this is not a definitive list, each cap included here tells its own story, revealing the diversity of design in modern cap culture.

OAKLAND RAIDERS VINTAGE PRO MODEL

CAPS: ONE SIZE FITS ALL

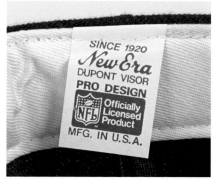

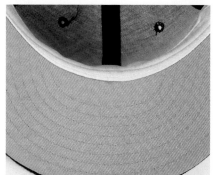

DATE: 1980S
CONSTRUCTION: 6-PANEL
FASTENER: FITTED

This vintage Raiders cap, produced by New Era in the USA, has the old-fashioned New Era labelling. Since the early 1990s, the Oakland Raiders team colours and uniform have become popular with the street fashion crowd. It's rumoured that the illustration of the player featured in the shield is a rendering of the actor Randolph Scott.

BROOKLYN BUSHWICKS 1949 AUTHENTIC BALLCAP

DATE: 2012
CONSTRUCTION: 6-PANEL
FASTENER: FITTED

Ebbets Field Flannels are known for creating caps with an authentic look that harks back to the early era of baseball. This example features a bold 'B' for the Brooklyn Bushwicks. This baseball club was the highest-ranking semi-pro team in New York during the first half of the 20th century, when semi-pro baseball was at its peak of popularity. This replica is constructed from wool, just like the original design, which dates back to 1949.

NEIGHBORHOOD KONA MESH

DATE: 2007
CONSTRUCTION: TRUCKER/5-PANEL
FASTENER: SNAPBACK

Neighborhood is a Japanese streetwear brand focusing on high-quality denim products. It was founded in 1994 by Shinsuke Takizawa. The label produces garments that feature the look of certain lifestyles, such as motorcyclists, rockabillies and military personnel. This limited-edition trucker-style cap has a mesh back with a snap closure. The foam-padded front panel features a Neighborhood brand patch. Inside the sweatband is a label with the words 'Fits All'.

TENDERLOIN LUMBERJACK

This is Japanese clothing brand Tenderloin's take on the classic American hunting cap. The insulated roll-down earflaps and crown protect the wearer from harsh weather conditions. Tenderloin also produced a jacket to match this cap.

DATE: 2006
CONSTRUCTION: 7-PIECE
FASTENER: FITTED

TENDERLOIN TRUCKER

DATE: 2007
CONSTRUCTION: TRUCKER
FASTENER: SNAPBACK

In 2007, Tenderloin used camouflage a great deal in their designs. For this cap, they sourced prewashed RealTee camouflage fabric direct from the USA. A custom brand patch and rope refinements are used on the crown. The cap was released in limited numbers.

STAPLE BAR LOGO

CAPS: ONE SIZE FITS ALL

In 1997, Jeff Staple founded the streetwear label Staple Design in New York City. The company also works as a creative consultancy studio and retailer overseeing the Lower East Side store Reed Space. Over the years, Staple Design has released various 5-panel caps. This example is from the early 2000s. It features Staple's bar logo at the front and the Staple 'S' on the leather strap. The words 'A Staple hat' are stitched under the brim. On the sweatband, nine quotations are printed on a label: '1. Open your heart; 2. Cleanse your soul; 3. Learn to love; 4. Tomorrow may never come; 5. Shine your light on the world; 6. A positive social contagion; 7. Staple Design; 8. Rinse; 9. Repeat'. The cap is constructed from cotton twill.

DATE: 2001
CONSTRUCTION: 5-PANEL
FASTENER: ADJUSTABLE LEATHER
STRAP

MASTERPIECE SOUND TING

DATE: 2006
CONSTRUCTION: TRUCKER
FASTENER: SNAPBACK

Masterpiece Sound is a reggae sound system based in Japan, and this cap displays the brand's appreciation of all things Jamaican. To create it, Masterpiece fashioned a pattern using an old Ting label (Ting is a popular soft drink in Jamaica). A sweater and footwear were produced to accompany the cap, which was released in small numbers and sold at selected stores globally. It is constructed from nylon, mesh and foam.

TREBARK TRUCKER

In 1972, Jim Crumley, a keen hunter from Buchanan, Virginia, felt that traditional military camouflage wasn't appropriate for hunting, and decided to dab splotches of brown dye on some grey work clothes to help him blend in better with his environment. After years of increased success in hunting, he refined this to a bark pattern, which was more accurately applied with a marker pen. Other hunters soon began to pester him for the new outfits, and in 1980, this original printed Trebark pattern was created. From then on, it became the unofficial dress code of the American hunter. This entire cap is covered in Trebark camouflage, including the nylon mesh.

DATE: 1980S
CONSTRUCTION: TRUCKER
FASTENER: SNAPBACK

AMBUSH DESIGN VVV STRAPBACK

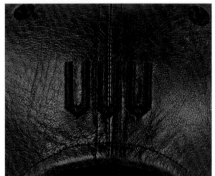

DATE: 2013
CONSTRUCTION: 6-PANEL
FASTENER: ADJUSTABLE LEATHER
STRAP

Tokyo-based brand Ambush Design released this luxurious cap in 2013. The front of the crown features skull, anarchy, star, moon and shield motifs. The cap is made from soft leather and has a leather strap closure.

NORSE PROJECTS X THE GOODHOOD STORE

DATE: 2012
CONSTRUCTION: 5-PANEL
FASTENER: NYLON WEBBED CLIP

This cap is a collaborative effort from Copenhagen-based label Norse Projects and The Goodhood Store in London, created to celebrate the shop's 5th anniversary. The black base with white polka dots signifies the dual branding, since polka dots are used in many of Goodhood's designs. Constructed from cotton twill, it was available from The Goodhood Store in limited numbers.

NORSE PROJECTS BEAVER

DATE: 2012
CONSTRUCTION: 5-PANEL
FASTENER: ADJUSTABLE LEATHER
STRAP

Norse Projects has released a number of caps since its inception in 2004. One popular model is their 5-panel cap; the beaver-print fabric in this example is sourced from the USA. The front of the crown features a brand information tag that bears the Norse Projects maxim, 'Created to improve life – Good for all seasons.'

NORSE PROJECTS X ERIK PARKER

DATE: 2013
CONSTRUCTION: 5-PANEL
FASTENER: NYLON WEBBED CLIP

Over the years, Norse Projects have collaborated with various stores and artists on their designs. On this cap they worked with the artist Erik Parker, taking imagery from his works to create an all-over print for the crown and brim. This cap was manufactured in the USA. The rear of the cap has a webbing closure, a system that is used in the majority of 5-panel caps.

STORMY KROMER

DATE: 2011 REPRODUCTION OF 1903 DESIGN

CONSTRUCTION: 6-PANEL

FASTENER: FITTED WITH PULLCORD

George 'Stormy' Kromer was a semi-pro baseball player who later worked as a railroad engineer. The story goes that every time he stuck his head out of his cabin window to see where his train was headed, the wind would blow his cap off. To solve this problem, he asked his wife, Ida, to modify an old baseball cap in a way that would help keep it on his head during windy weather. The design she came up with had laces at the front that the wearer could pull to tighten the cap.

The original Stormy Kromer cap was made of cloth with a canvas visor; it was a departure from the traditional felt fedoras of the day, but it was also more comfortable. Other workers expressed an interest in the cap, so Kromer took on some employees and began to manufacture it professionally. The entire cap, which is made of cotton, has been paraffin-waxed, making it water-resistant. The design also comes in wool for the winter.

WTAPS '96-'69 DERBY

WTAPS was established by Tetsu Nishiyama in the Harajuku district of Tokyo in 1996. The label's design philosophy is inspired by that of traditional Japanese carpenters, who use every bit of the wood they work with and ensure that nothing is wasted. To create this cap, WTAPS removed the traditional bowler (or derby) hat brim and replaced it with a peaked visor. The crown is made from flexible felt. The interior contains a WTAPS information tag and an embroidered label that reads 'Placing things where they should be'. It was only available from WTAPS stockists and was produced in limited numbers.

DATE: 2010
CONSTRUCTION: DERBY
FASTENER: FITTED

WTAPS CHE

DATE: 2005
CONSTRUCTION: FATIGUE/FIELD
FASTENER: FITTED

Since WTAPS' inception it has frequently appropriated military-style silhouettes. On this occasion, it adapted the traditional flat-top cap design and used it in conjunction with WTAPS' teardrop pattern, which is embroidered, rather than printed, all over the cap. A majority of the brand's clothing features its trademark red tab; it makes an appearance here on the right-hand side of the crown. The cap is constructed from soft cotton, was only available from WTAPS stockists and was produced in limited numbers.

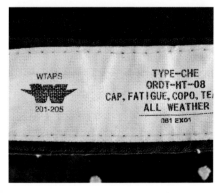

PATTA X NEW ERA

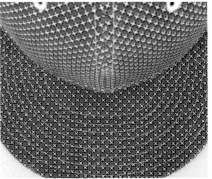

DATE: 2007
CONSTRUCTION: 6-PANEL
FASTENER: FITTED

This was the first cap that renowned Amsterdam-based streetwear brand Patta produced with New Era. It was part of a Patta x ASICS Gel Lyte III shoe release; the pattern and colours used on the cap correlated with parts of the trainers. The crown is decorated with Patta's cross and square pattern and contrasting stitching. The underside of the brim is green, which matches the embroidered green Patta logo on the side. This cap was available exclusively at the Patta store at first and then was distributed globally.

PATTA 'GOT LOVE FOR ALL'

DATE: 2012
CONSTRUCTION: 6-PANEL
FASTENER: FITTED

To create this fitted wool cap, Patta worked with vintage manufacturers Ebbets Field. The crown features Patta's logo and the slogan 'Got Love for All' in contrasting black stitching. Black symbols of peace and love are stitched around the crown.

COCA-COLA LONG-BILL

CAPS: ONE SIZE FITS ALL

DATE: 1990S
CONSTRUCTION: 5-PANEL
FASTENER: DRAWSTRING

Coca-Cola produced these long-bill cotton caps as a promotional item in the 1990s, when Coca-Cola apparel was popular among hip-hop enthusiasts. Key design features, such as the multicoloured 5-panel construction with a drawstring adjustment at the back, make this cap a cult classic. The drawstring was particularly unusual at the time it was released.

VANS SYNDICATE

DATE: 2012
CONSTRUCTION: 6-PANEL
FASTENER: SNAPBACK

Shoe brand Vans was established in California in 1966, and is still hugely popular today. Founder Paul Van Doren quickly saw his shoes being adopted by the skate community. Over the years, Vans began to produce caps as well as shoes. In 2012, Starter produced this one as part of the Vans Syndicate series; this black-and-white version was dropped from the retail market. Some say that the word 'Syndicate' embroidered on this cotton cap refers to hip-hop collective the Rhyme Syndicate, of which Ice-T was a member.

SUBWARE 'S'

Stash, founder of legendary clothing design studio Subware, exhibited his first canvases at a group show at New York's Fun Gallery in 1983, alongside works by Pop art pioneers Keith Haring and Jean-Michel Basquiat, when he was just 17 years old. In 1985, his piece *The Wall* was published in Henry Chalfant and James Prigoff's renowned graffiti book *Spraycan Art*. By the late 1990s, Stash had pioneered the use of graffiti's graphic elements on streetwear garments through high-profile collaborations with companies including Nike, Medicom, Gravis and A Bathing Ape. This cap features the Subware 'S' logo embedded in a Superman-style emblem that is stitched into the crown. The rear has an adjustable snapback closure. Constructed from wool, it was released in limited numbers and was only available from selected stores.

DATE: 2002
CONSTRUCTION: 6-PANEL
FASTENER: SNAPBACK

ZOO YORK HAROLD HUNTER 59FIFTY

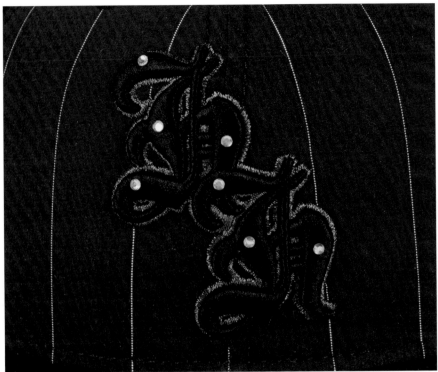

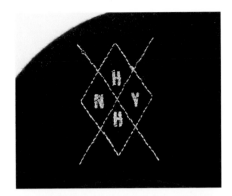

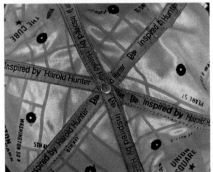

DATE: 2006
CONSTRUCTION: 6-PANEL
FASTENER: FITTED

New York based skateboarding brand Zoo York worked together with New Era to create this special cap commemorating the life of skater Harold Hunter. The Old English 'HH' (for Harold Hunter) in studs on the crown is a homage to one of Harold's early Zoo York graphics. The cap, constructed from black cashmere, has pinstriped front panels; a quote from Harold is embroidered inside the sweatband, and the letters 'HH/NY' appear under the brim. It also has a yellow satin lining with a map of Harold's favourite skate locations in New York. Each cap was packaged in a satin-lined wooden box, and only 288 were produced. The proceeds from the sale of the caps went to Stoked Mentoring.

SLAM CITY SKATES QUILTED

DATE: 2009
CONSTRUCTION: 6-PANEL
FASTENER: FITTED

Slam City Skates is a skateboarding shop located in the heart of London. In 2009, it released a series of fitted caps manufactured by New Era. The quilted crown and corduroy brim were inspired by classic Barbour jackets, and just like the jackets, the inside of the cap had a silky lining. A large 3D embroidered 'S', for Slam City Skates, appears on the crown. This cap was only available from the Slam City shop.

PALACE BLAZERS

DATE: 2012
CONSTRUCTION: 5-PANEL
FASTENER: SNAPBACK

This was the first snapback cap released by London collective Palace Skateboards; they were manufactured by Ebbets Field. The inspiration for it was the logo and typography of the Portland Trail Blazers, hence its nickname, the 'Blazers' cap'. There are rumoured to have been only 500 made, and they were constructed from cotton.

PALACE X EBBETS FIELD FLANNELS

CAPS: ONE SIZE FITS ALL

DATE: 2012
CONSTRUCTION: 6-PANEL
FASTENER: ADJUSTABLE LEATHER
STRAP

Ebbets Field Flannels produced this cap for Palace Skateboards. The front features an embroidered appliqué 'P'. It is made from wool with an adjustable leather strap closure. Like all Ebbets Field products, this cap was manufactured in the USA. It came in 4 colours: white, green, navy and red. Only 50 of each colour were made.

BAPE (A BATHING APE) FITTED CORDUROY

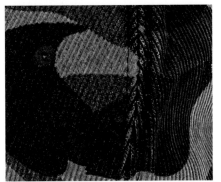

DATE: 2002

CONSTRUCTION: 6-PANEL

FASTENER: FITTED

A Bathing Ape (or BAPE) was founded by the music producer and DJ Nigo in Tokyo in 1994. The brand's interpretation of the Korean army's camouflage pattern has become one of the most widely recognized prints in the streetwear world. BAPE had previously produced many caps featuring this pattern, but this is the only one made of corduroy. This cap was manufactured by BAPE; after 2002 the brand began to sell caps that had been produced by New Era and Ebbets Field.

BAPE FOOT SOLDIER

DATE: 2005

CONSTRUCTION: 6-PANEL

FASTENER: FITTED

A Bathing Ape produced this fitted wool cap as part of their collection for the BAPE-owned trainer store Foot Soldier. The black and grey crown features a BAPE emblem on the left and Foot Soldier silhouettes, also known as BAPE Troopers, on the right. White piping separates the panels, and a wordmark is stitched on the rear. This fitted cap was only available at BAPE stores.

BOUNTY HUNTER NAVAL

Bounty Hunter, a label from Tokyo, created its own unique version of a naval cap that uses soft-engineered mesh at the back of the crown. The brand's sense of humour is evident on the washing instructions label, which reads 'Do Not Breach' and 'Do Not Be Stupid'.

DATE: 2000S
CONSTRUCTION: TRUCKER 5-PANEL
FASTENER: SNAPBACK

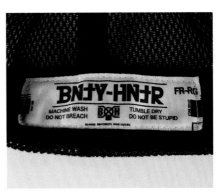

CAPS: ONE SIZE FITS ALL

NIKE TAILWIND

DATE: 1999
CONSTRUCTION: 5-PANEL
FASTENER: NYLON WEBBED CLIP

Over the years Nike has continued to perfect its running caps, and this 5-panel cap is part of that journey. The shape and colours complemented the popular high-tech footwear of the late 1990s and the Tailwind was adopted by the street fashion crowd. This was the first time Nike had used reflective material on a running cap. The clip closure and Nike Clima-FIT fabric were also new features.

CASSETTE PLAYA CHIMERAS

CAPS: ONE SIZE FITS ALL

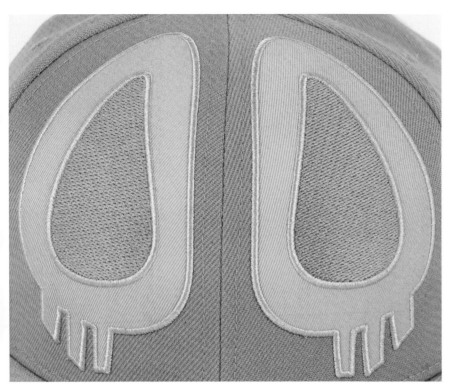

DATE: 2008

CONSTRUCTION: 6-PANEL

FASTENER: SNAPBACK

Nike produced this vibrant snapback with British fashion designer Carri Munden (aka Cassette Playa). It showcases her futuristic, colourful and glitchy aesthetic, and the phrase 'Fear No Evil' is embroidered on the back. The cap was created exclusively for a Cassette Playa fashion show, was named after a fictional sports team and was never available in stores.

UXA CAMOUFLAGE

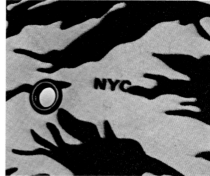

DATE: 2003
CONSTRUCTION: 5-PANEL
FASTENER: NYLON ADJUSTABLE STRAP

UXA, a skateboarding brand from New York City, was founded by passionate skateboarders Jeff Pang, Peter Bici and Peter Huynh in 2000. In 2003, UXA released this 5-panel cotton cap with UXA's own custom camouflage design. It came in various colourways but was limited to an edition of 100.

UNDEFEATED CYCLING

In 2002 Eddie Cruz and James Bond created the footwear store Undefeated and opened their first branch in Los Angeles. The brand turned a standard New Era cap on its head with this cycling-inspired design. Iconic cycling logos and trademarks have been remixed to give this cap a real classic cycling look. The rear of the crown features the UCI championship colours, which are often seen on cycling apparel. Undefeated are obviously fans of Cinelli and Eddy Merckx, since both logos are the inspiration for the designs on the crown and brim. This cap was only released in Undefeated stores in limited numbers.

DATE: 2008
CONSTRUCTION: 6-PANEL
FASTENER: FITTED

UNDEFEATED U-MAN

DATE: 2002
CONSTRUCTION: 6-PANEL
FASTENER: FITTED

This cap is one of Undefeated's first releases, and features its U-Man logo. 'Undefeated' is also stitched onto the side panel, and the UNDFTD label appears inside. The design was released in limited quantities and was only available at Undefeated stores.

UNDEFEATED SPLATTER 59FIFTY

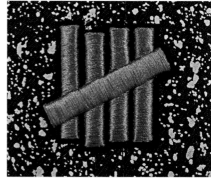

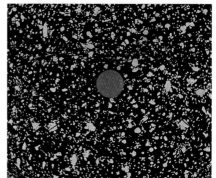

DATE: EARLY 2000S
CONSTRUCTION: 6-PANEL
FASTENER: FITTED

Undefeated released this cap in conjunction with their Nike Dunk shoe. The Dunk incorporated a paint-splattered pattern that has been replicated on the cap. New Era produced this cap and it was released in 2 colourways. They were only available from Undefeated stores.

SUPREME X RAMMELLZEE

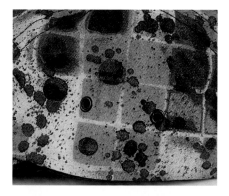

DATE: 2004
CONSTRUCTION: 5-PANEL
FASTENER: NYLON WEBBED CLIP

In 2004, Supreme collaborated with Rammellzee, an influential hip-hop pioneer from New York who began as a rapper in the 1980s but eventually turned to making art. These caps were part of a collection that was all hand-sprayed and customized by the artist in his signature style. The 5-panel caps were produced in 2 colourways and released in limited numbers.

SUPREME ELEPHANT PRINT

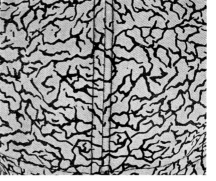

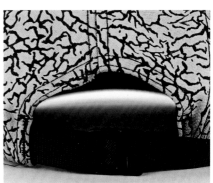

DATE: 2002
CONSTRUCTION: 5-PANEL
FASTENER: NYLON WEBBED CLIP

In 2002, Supreme partnered with Nike for the first time to produce a collaborative take on a classic basketball shoe. Supreme released 2 elephant-print caps, inspired by the iconic Jordan III cement pattern from 1988, to match the colours of 2 styles of limited-edition shoes. The Air Jordan series has a fair share of fanatics, and they're particularly obsessed with seeking out this hat.

SUPREME X COMME DES GARÇONS SHIRT

DATE: 2012
CONSTRUCTION: 5-PANEL
FASTENER: NYLON WEBBED CLIP

Supreme and Comme des Garçons SHIRT came together to create this 5-panel cap, part of a capsule collection designed to coincide with the opening of a Tokyo-based Dover Street Market store in Ginza. Supreme used Comme des Garçons SHIRT's signature pinstriped fabric on this design. These caps were produced in 3 styles and were available in limited numbers from all Supreme stores and from Dover Street Market outlets in London and Tokyo.

SUPREME X NEIGHBORHOOD 59FIFTY

DATE: 2006
CONSTRUCTION: 6-PANEL
FASTENER: FITTED

Two heavyweight brands came together to create this truly exciting cap, produced by New Era. The crown is covered in monotone printed stars. Its main focus is the large embroidered emblem featuring the words 'Humanity, Justice, Freedom', which flows from the crown to the brim. The cap was released in 4 colours in very limited numbers as part of a collection that included T-shirts, denim and a jacket.

ANYTHING (A NEW YORK THING) SUNRISE

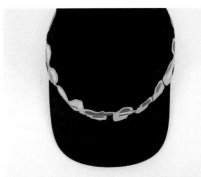

DATE: 2006
CONSTRUCTION: PAINTER'S
FASTENER: FITTED

During the 1980s the painter's cap was a popular choice for promotional use. Skateboard and BMX teams were early adopters, since the large panels were a perfect blank canvas on which to print designs. This space has been well utilized on this cap, with extra-large 'ANYTHING' lettering around the crown leaving little mystery as to who made it.

ANYTHING MESH

DATE: 2008
CONSTRUCTION: TRUCKER 5-PANEL
FASTENER: SNAPBACK

In the past, trucker caps were unpopular because they softened over time. In this take on a trucker cap, aNYthing constructed the whole crown from mesh instead of using the traditional foam front. It was released in a variety of colours.

HUF REFLECTIVE

DATE: 2007
CONSTRUCTION: 6-PANEL
FASTENER: FITTED

San Francisco-based brand Huf released a series of fitted caps made from reflective material, which New Era produced in 4 different colours. They were created to coincide with the Huf x DVS shoe project called the 3M Pack. The whole crown and peak give a hi-vis effect at night, handy when skateboarding. These caps were released in limited numbers.

ODD FUTURE GOLF

DATE: 2012
CONSTRUCTION: 5-PANEL
FASTENER: SNAPBACK

In 2012, Los Angeles hip-hop collective Odd Future released a collection of snapback caps. In this example, the 'Golf' lettering across the front is styled in a gothic font. A small cat is stitched into the side panel to the left of the snapback closure. Cats are a recurring motif in Odd Future's clothing line. The Golf cap, which was constructed from cotton, was released in a variety of colours.

MARVEL COMICS THOR-MATIC

DATE: 2010
CONSTRUCTION: 6-PANEL
FASTENER: FITTED

New Era and comic book legends Marvel collaborated on a range of caps called the Heroes Collection. This cap is from the Thor-Matic series. The crown panels and brim feature a print of Marvel's comic-strip artwork and an embroidered Marvel Comics logo is stitched into the rear of the fitted cap. New Era also produced a black-and-white version of this cap. Both were available from New Era's stores.

CAMPAGNOLO HERITAGE

DATE: 2005
CONSTRUCTION: 2-PIECE
FASTENER: ELASTICATED

The Italian bicycle-part manufacturer Campagnolo is classed as one of the most prestigious in the world. Founded in Vicenza in 1933 by Commendatore Tullio Campagnolo, the company has created countless cycling caps over its 80-year history. The example here is a classic model made from cotton that features the UCI championship colour trim over the crown. This trim is not only for decoration but supports the hat. An elasticated rear keeps the cap firmly on the head.

MERCIAN CYCLING

DATE: 2006
CONSTRUCTION: 2-PIECE
FASTENER: ELASTICATED

Mercian Cycles are a small independent cycle company based in Derbyshire, UK, who have been hand-building bespoke bicycle frames since 1946. This cap is rare, since it was released in small numbers and was only available from the Mercian workshop. Made from cotton, it features the Mercian typeface on the brim and the side panels of the cap. It has an elasticated rear for fitting. It was made in England by Impsport, who produced custom cycling apparel.

SAN FRANCISCO 49ERS

DATE: 1992

CONSTRUCTION: 6-PANEL

FASTENER: SNAPBACK

The main feature of this cap is the large San Francisco 49ers logo that is stitched onto the crown, while the NFL logo is printed on the side panel. Pro One, the manufacturer, has its logo on the rear.

NEW YORK YANKEES AUTHENTIC ON-FIELD GAME 59FIFTY

DATE: 2012
CONSTRUCTION: 6-PANEL
FASTENER: FITTED

The Authentic Collection 59FIFTY is the official on-field cap of Major League Baseball: since 1954 every MLB team has worn them. The cap was made available to the public in 1978. Constructed in polyester, it features New Era's CoolBase technology, which is moisture-wicking, quick drying and shrink-resistant. The cap is available in various sizes. The crown has an embroidered and raised New York Yankees team logo on the front and a stitched MLB logo on the rear. Inside there is branded taping and a black sweatband.

ACAPULCO GOLD ANGRY 'LO BEAR

CAPS: ONE SIZE FITS ALL

DATE: 2012
CONSTRUCTION: 6-PANEL
FASTENER: SNAPBACK

The cotton twill crown of this cap features Acapulco Gold's Angry 'Lo Bear character, the infamous bear brandishing a baseball bat that often features on their clothing and accessories. The corduroy brim complements the crown. The company's branding is also present on the red tab on the snapback closure. Acapulco Gold produced this design in 3 colours: navy, burgundy and black.

GEORGETOWN HOYAS

DATE: EARLY 1990S
CONSTRUCTION: 6-PANEL
FASTENER: SNAPBACK

Blue and grey are the official colours of Georgetown University and its athletic teams. There have been numerous editions of the Georgetown Hoyas cap; some have featured the Hoyas' mascot, Jack the bulldog, while others have simply carried the serifed letter 'G' for Georgetown. This example, produced by Starter, features the word 'Georgetown' in a block-style font. This style of lettering has been imitated on hundreds of caps.

MIGHTY DUCKS

DATE: 1993
CONSTRUCTION: 6-PANEL
FASTENER: SNAPBACK

The Walt Disney Company founded the professional ice hockey team Mighty Ducks of Anaheim in 1993, naming them after their *The Mighty Ducks* movie of the previous year. Starter was the only company licenced by Disney to produce Mighty Ducks apparel for retail. However, other companies produced Mighty Ducks clothing when the licence ended, and Disney eventually sold the franchise in 2005. This snapback cap is made from cotton; it features the Mighty Ducks hockey-mask logo on the crown.

TRAPSTAR SIGNATURE

CAPS: ONE SIZE FITS ALL

DATE: 2007

CONSTRUCTION: 6-PANEL

FASTENER: SNAPBACK

A huge array of independent lifestyle brands are based in London, but not many of them have had Trapstar's success in having their products embraced by celebrities in just a short period of time. In 2012, pop star Rihanna was photographed countless times wearing one of Trapstar's caps. This is the first cap Trapstar ever produced; it was released in limited quantities and was only available from the brand's online store. It features Trapstar's signature script logo across the crown.

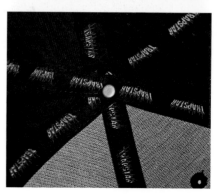

HARTFORD WHALERS 'THE SWIRL'

DATE: 2013
CONSTRUCTION: 6-PANEL
FASTENER: SNAPBACK

Mitchell & Ness have played a huge part in reintroducing the snapback to the mainstream cap market. This Hartford Whalers cap paid homage to the vintage snapback era with its tri-coloured swirl design. The colours are those of the Hartford Whalers ice hockey team. It features a raised embroidered Hartford Whalers logo on the right panel and 2-toned Whalers lettering over the top of the crown. The Mitchell & Ness logo appears above the snapback closure.

ESPN 'BOO-YEAH!!'

DATE: 1996
CONSTRUCTION: 6-PANEL
FASTENER: ADJUSTABLE COTTON STRAP

This cap is a promotional item for the US TV network ESPN; it was only available on studio tours. It features the network's 'Boo-Yeah!!' strapline stitched onto the rear; this was a well-known catchphrase of *SportCenter* anchor Stuart Scott. The cap has an adjustable strap and is constructed from cotton twill.

MARVIN THE MARTIAN

DATE: 1991
CONSTRUCTION: 6-PANEL
FASTENER: FITTED

This cap, produced by the ACME Clothing Co., features Marvin the Martian, a popular *Looney Tunes* character created by Chuck Jones. Marvin made his debut in 1948. On this cap he cleverly features in embroidered details on the front and rear of the crown.

ATLANTA 1996 OLYMPICS

DATE: 1996
CONSTRUCTION: 5-PANEL
FASTENER: SNAPBACK

Avon Products, Inc., from New York, released their Olympic Game Collection for the 1996 Atlanta Games. They produced a series of cap memorabilia; this snapback features the Atlanta Games' flame logo on the front of the crown.

WU-TANG CLAN X ALIFE

CAPS: ONE SIZE FITS ALL

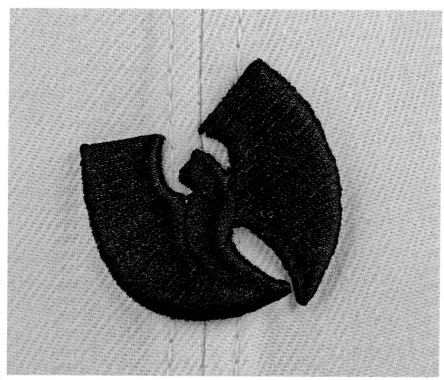

DATE: 2006
CONSTRUCTION: 6-PANEL
FASTENER: FITTED

New York collective alife used this collaborative project to pay homage to the Wu-Tang Clan. The front of the crown features their infamous 'W' symbol, and 'alife' is embroidered on the side panel. This cap, produced by New Era, was released in red, white and yellow; the yellow was the most memorable of the 3, as black and yellow are the Wu-Tang Clan's signature colours.

STONE ISLAND REFLECTIVE LOGO

DATE: 2013

CONSTRUCTION: 5-PANEL
FASTENER: NYLON WEBBED CLIP

Since its humble launch in 1982, Stone Island has been on a mission to create innovative designs. Constantly reimagining the possibilities of materials and fabrics, they have broken down boundaries in manufacturing. Their interest in the functionality of a garment is also always evident. This 5-panel cotton cap features a reflective Stone Island compass logo. It can be fitted with the adjustable clip closure.

POLO RALPH LAUREN CLASSIC SPORT

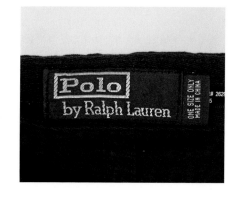

DATE: 2009
CONSTRUCTION: 6-PANEL
FASTENER: ADJUSTABLE LEATHER
STRAP

Since the 1980s, Ralph Lauren's signature cap has been a staple of the company's headwear collection, and has been sold in huge numbers around the world. Made in countless colours, it is worn by both men and women. The design was originally taken from a vintage driving cap. The 'POLO' on the rear complements the Ralph Lauren logo on the crown. It is constructed from durable washed cotton twill and kept secure with a leather strap closure.

DKNY USA EQUIPMENT

DATE: 1997
CONSTRUCTION: 6-PANEL
FASTENER: NYLON ADJUSTABLE STRAP
WITH CLIP

In 1997, DKNY (Donna Karan New York) ventured into sportswear; this 6-panel cap was part of the brand's initial offering. DKNY used breathable nylon, since the cap was specifically meant to be worn during sporting activities. It was released in a variety of colours, was only available in DKNY stores and featured a clip closure.

CHAMPION USA CHECKED

DATE: 1990
CONSTRUCTION: 12-PANEL
FASTENER: SNAPBACK

This Champion USA snapback has an unusual 12-panel crown construction. A large logo is embroidered on the front panel of this rayon cap, and the underside of the brim is green. The adjustable plastic closure controls the sizing.

MARC JACOBS PARIS 59FIFTY

CAPS: ONE SIZE FITS ALL

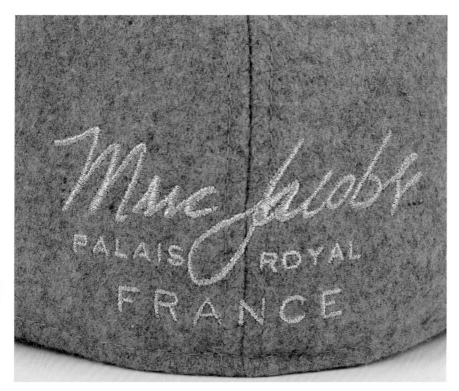

DATE: 2011
CONSTRUCTION: 6-PANEL
FASTENER: FITTED

New York-based fashion label Marc Jacobs designed 3 caps that were produced by the New Era Cap Co. The team chose the 59FIFTY fitted cap, as its origins are from Major League Baseball. The 3 caps were made from different shades of grey wool, and the fronts of the crowns featured the words 'PARIS', 'NEW YORK' and 'MJ' in embroidered script. Rumour has it that the first 2 caps named locations where Marc Jacobs has had homes.

KUWAIT NAVAL FORCE

DATE: 2000S
CONSTRUCTION: 6-PANEL
FASTENER: SNAPBACK

Members of the Kuwait Naval Force wore this wool cap during the war against Iraq. The words 'KUWAIT NAVAL FORCE – Be confident We are On WATCH!' are embroidered on it in golden cotton, together with a multicoloured image of a naval vessel flying the Kuwaiti flag with minarets in the background. Gold oak leaves and acorns are machine-embroidered on the brim.

MISHKA KEEP WATCH AVIATOR

DATE: 2008
CONSTRUCTION: 5-PANEL WITH EAR
FLAPS
FASTENER: FITTED

Clothing label Mishka NYC was established in the early 2000s and is recognized for its unorthodox designs, in which the eyeball logo, called 'Keep Watch', has played a huge part. This cap, manufactured by New Era, is no exception. The ear flaps and crown are made of PU leather, while the interior uses fake fur to keep the head warm. A metal fastening secures the ear flaps when they are not in use. This cap was only available from Mishka stockists.

STUSSY GOLD GIRLS GLORY

CAPS: ONE SIZE FITS ALL

DATE: 2006
CONSTRUCTION: 6-PANEL
FASTENER: FITTED

All the apparel in Stussy's collection Gold Girls Glory featured the collection's name, printed in the iconic Shawn Stussy script. The caps, however, had the words embroidered around the crown. They were produced in a variety of colourways.

STUSSY MILITARY FLAT-TOP BDU CAMOUFLAGE

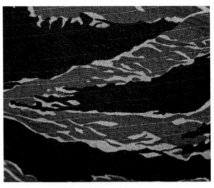

DATE: 2005

CONSTRUCTION: FLAT-TOP

FASTENER: ADJUSTABLE VELCRO

Stussy have produced more styles than most when it comes to headwear. In 2005, they released this military-inspired cap in a Vietnamese tiger-stripe camouflage pattern. The military theme continues with a replica data patch on the front of the crown. The cap is made from durable Ripstock cotton.

STUSSY STAND FIRM

DATE: 2008
CONSTRUCTION: 6-PANEL
FASTENER: FITTED

Stussy have an array of slogans and statements that are used on their clothing and campaigns. For this cap, 'Stand Firm' is the slogan of choice, and the words are embroidered in large letters around the crown. This cap was released in various colours.

STUSSY WORLDWIDE 59FIFTY

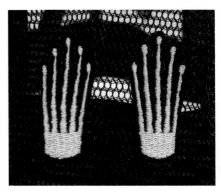

DATE: 2000
CONSTRUCTION: 6-PANEL
FASTENER: FITTED

This was one of Stussy's first fitted mesh caps. The rear mesh panel features Stussy Tribe location badges, each representing a Stussy store around the world. Also on the mesh panel is the Stussy logo. New Era produced this cap for Stussy. It was released in 3 colours and was only available at Stussy stores.

BROOKLYN BASEMENTS REFLECTIVE LONG-BILL

Hunted for and deified by collectors of vintage Ralph Lauren pieces, long-bill caps represent a particular era in style. Brooklyn Basements label founder Tommy Rebel is a world-renowned Ralph Lauren collector, and photos of his impressive collection have been the stuff of legend on vintage collector forums. His hats gained so much attention that Rebel was offered a serious amount of cash to sell the entire collection. After taking the offer, he decided to craft his own version of the legendary long-bill cap. However, he advanced the aesthetic a step further by using reflective material, and produced the cap alongside a series of equally eye-catching jackets. These caps were made in limited quantities and were only available from Brooklyn Basements in New York.

DATE: 2005
CONSTRUCTION: 5-PANEL
FASTENER: ELASTICATED

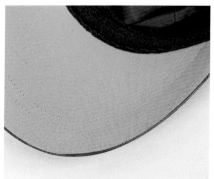

MILWAUKEE BREWERS PAINTER'S CAP

DATE: 1990S
CONSTRUCTION: PAINTER'S
FASTENER: ELASTICATED

This painter's cap was produced by Twins Enterprises, Inc., Boston. Painter's caps are a cheaper alternative to baseball caps. Another advantage is that you can print over a larger surface area of painter's caps; this one has large logos on the top and front, which isn't possible on a regular baseball cap.

FELIX THE CAT PAINTER'S CAP

DATE: 1982
CONSTRUCTION: PAINTER'S
FASTENER: ELASTICATED

This cotton painter's cap was made in early 1982. It features Felix the Cat, a black-and-white cartoon cat character with a big grin who was created in the silent film era and is one of the most recognized cartoon characters in film history. Images of Felix in various poses appear around the crown.

CHICAGO WHITE SOX PAINTER'S SNAPBACK

DATE: 1980

CONSTRUCTION: PAINTER'S

FASTENER: SNAPBACK

This cap features a snapback closure; this is rare for a painter's cap, the majority of which have elastic at the rear. The batter silhouette logo over the 'SOX' wordmark dates from 1976. The White Sox stopped using this logo during the late 1980s.

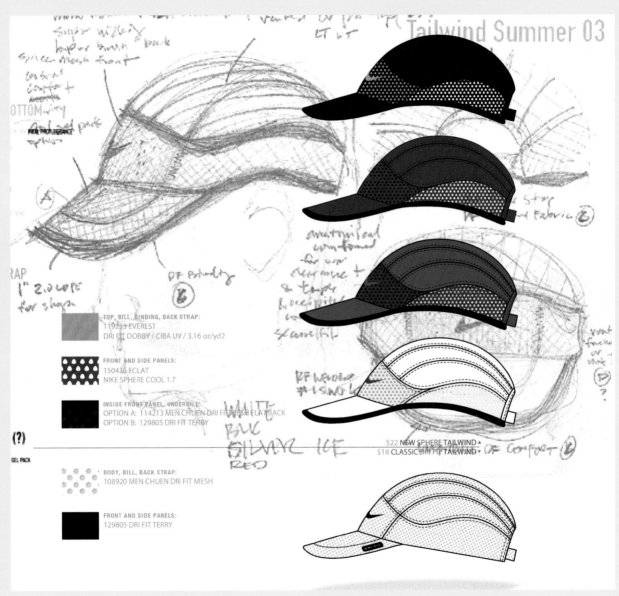

Former Nike headwear designer Jon Taguchi's sketches for the company's Tailwind cap, 2002.

INFLUENCERS AND INNOVATORS

This section features interviews with key insiders from the streetwear world who have taken the cap from workwear and sporting staple to downright desirable accessory. They include creators whose innovative ideas have pushed forward cap design; influencers that brought niche labels to new markets; collectors whose stash will induce envy among the street fashion crowd; cultural reporters that are first off the bat when a new design drops; and connoisseurs who can spot when a trend is about to blow up. Each of them has made a unique contribution to cap culture. Here these key players reveal when they started wearing caps, the best brands currently in the game, the caps they wished they had copped and their opinions on how cap culture has developed – and where it is heading.

DJ CLARK

Clark Kent, aka DJ Clark, is a hip-hop DJ, record producer and music executive. He's produced music for rap legends Jay-Z, Notorious B.I.G., 50 Cent, Slick Rick and Rakim. With over 20 years in the music industry, Clark has witnessed the constant changes in hip-hop fashion. He's also a well-known sneaker connoisseur, with a collection numbering in the thousands – and he's got a huge collection of caps to match.

Can you tell me when your relationship with the baseball cap first started?

It started when I was around 9 years old and playing Little League baseball. I'm sure my mother or grandmother put me in baseball caps before that. But I can remember having a cap at Little League as I played. I can't remember the look of the cap, but I remember the team was called the Pirates from Brooklyn. My first fitted cap was a Yankees cap.

How does it make you feel that the New York Yankees cap is one of the most recognized baseball caps in the world?

That 'NY' is the most iconic baseball symbol: there's nothing more recognizable in American sports. Every team wishes they could be as important as the Yankees. I'm a super Giants fan, but the Yankees have so much amazing history behind them. The 'NY' speaks for New York, the centre of the universe.

How many caps do you own?

I might have about 1,200 left.

Where do you store them all?

I have racks and storage shelves that keep them in shape. They're stacked, as you would see them in a store.

What's your favourite style of cap?

The New Era fitted: I like the way they fit. They're iconic.

Why do you wear caps?

I like the way they look. My love and admiration for the cap is a style thing: it's how the cap looks, it's part of your daily uniform. I'm from New York, so the cap added a little 'sinister-ism': you could use it to hide your face. It leaves people asking what's going on under the brim.

What's your favourite cap?

I have 2: the New Era NY Yankee Cooperstown Classic on-field cap with green under the bill and the New Era Jackie Robinson Brooklyn Dodgers Cooperstown Classic, also with green under the bill.

Who do you feel produces the best caps?

No question, it's the New Era Cap Co.

Is there any cap you wanted that you never had?

Yeah, the CLOT x New Era Red silk that matches the CLOT Nike Air Force 1. I have the shoes, and I like how they match them. The fabrics are so similar.

Where do you get your caps?

I go all over the place. The New Era store in NYC is where I always get my Yankees and Brooklyn Dodgers caps.

Have you found anything interesting on your travels?

Every time I go to Japan I find something special that I'm not going to see in the USA. The New Era store in Japan has insane caps. They had a Mickey Mouse fitted cap, which I liked so much that I bought it in every colour they had. A Mickey Mouse New Era is special.

Do you think you will eventually stop wearing caps?

No, I don't think so. I like them too much. They're part of my uniform.

Why do you think the cap is so important in today's street culture?

I think purely for style. True hip-hop derives from the street. Fashion statements come from the street first, then hip-hop borrows them and makes them its own. The cap is going to stay relevant as brands keep making them; the idea of having caps that match something is always going to be important.

F AS IN FRANK

F As In Frank, run by siblings Jesse and Drew Heifetz, is a cap-centric approach to the vintage sportswear shopping experience. The Heifetz brothers were born into the world of used and deadstock clothing via their father, David, who helped pioneer the family business in the late 1960s. Wholesaling as well as hoarding for their own private collections, Jesse and Drew's F As In Frank store opened in Whistler, Canada, in 2007, before an escalating cult following led to a larger Vancouver location and a space in Toronto. Buying and selling in substantial quantities, the Heifetz brothers' Canadian ventures are key destinations for cap connoisseurs and casual fans looking for elusive colours or designs.

How long have you been selling vintage caps?

Since about 2005. Back then, there was nobody else really doing it. We were travelling all over the US and Canada, buying up all the hats we could find dirt cheap. The customers at that point were a very select crowd. We would do pop-up shops in New York and LA, and really we were just hustling. We didn't open our first store until 2007.

Which style of cap is your most popular seller?

Over the years, different styles come and go. When we first started buying caps, we were passing up shark-tooth and splash snapbacks all the time because no one wanted them. Now they are the hottest sellers. But overall, the Sports Specialties script hat is and will always be the most collectible and sought-after snapback. It is so classic and timeless. You can find them on every celebrity and professional athlete from the 1980s and '90s.

Which are the most popular team caps?

Raiders, Bulls and Kings are the most desirable teams as far as vintage clothing and snapbacks go. In the last few years, the Mighty Ducks have become super popular for collectors. One reason for this is that Disney owns the rights to the Ducks, so no company has been able to produce retro Ducks gear. This keeps the demand high for the true vintage pieces.

Has there been a change in the type of customer that purchases caps?

A huge change! Back in 2007, only true vintage-heads were into it. The customers then were a bit older. They were guys who remembered when the gear they were wearing had been worn by their favourite musician or athlete. Once the craze kicked in around 2009, the customers completely switched. Celebrities started to rock vintage gear and snapbacks and it made them desirable to all the swag kids. Now we sell snapbacks to kids who are 13 or 14. The culture around caps has completely changed.

When did the popularity of vintage caps begin?

It started for the original vintage buyers in about 2007 but hit the mainstream in about 2010. In 2010, New Era went from selling 100 per cent fitted caps to selling 50 per cent fitteds and 50 per cent snapbacks – in one year. That is pretty unheard of. Now they sell 90 per cent snapbacks. When the trend hit hard, we already had a huge warehouse filled with vintage snapbacks. It was hard to see it coming.

What are your top 3 favourite caps?

Sports Specialties leather script strapbacks, the Starter Image Series and the White Sox blockhead.

Do you think the cap is an important part of today's fashion?

We think that the hat is very important. There are so many different hats out there that you can find one that fits most outfits. You can rock an Ivy League college game snapback with a nice shirt, cardigan and trousers for that collegiate look, or throw on your Mighty Ducks shark-tooth with a bleached-out denim vest and turquoise sneakers for a more fresh on Fairfax look.

MISTER MORT

Born and raised a Hasidic Jew, Mordechai Rubinstein attended rabbinical school in Israel before relocating to New York City in 1994. He worked as a publicist at clothing label Jack Spade before moving on to *Men's Vogue* as a fashion market-trend researcher. His time there exposed him to the personalities that make up the industry, and as Mister Mort he has since become an exceptional fashion blogger with a keen eye for detail. He founded his blog in 2008 as a way to organize his collection of street style photographs. As well as snapping people's shoes and clothing, he has documented various caps as worn by an eclectic cast of characters. His blog features a wide range of subjects, from NYC uniformed police, to down-and-out Bowery residents, to his artist friends.

How long have you been wearing caps?

I'm not sure of the exact age, but growing up wearing a yarmulke, I often topped it off with a cap when going to ball games or amusement parks. I started wearing a fedora at 13, but still preferred a cap to the young-looking rabbi uniform (I thought that kind of looked like a costume on a young fella). In 10th grade, my principal Rabbi Thaler confiscated all my caps. I had caps for every American League and most National League teams and the Yeshiva (school) did not permit caps, even in physical education class. That really set me back and I haven't completely recovered. I still think about the way those USA-made New Eras wore – today's caps are polyester and don't break in in the same way.

What is your favourite type of cap?

Probably a classic on-field New Era fitted baseball cap. While I love many different type of hats – like classic buckets, Greek fishermen's hats and beanies – most people confuse caps with hats. I know the difference.

What's your earliest cap memory?

I think my earliest memory of a favourite cap was when I was convinced to ride the rollercoaster at an amusement park. As soon as it went upside down, my cap fell off, and I watched it fly down like a propeller. I never saw it again. It was a size 6¾ fitted Boston Celtics cap, and it was a gift from my younger brother Moshe. While we weren't really sports fans, we did have favourite teams. For me, it was always about the logo or colour of a uniform rather than a specific player or how a team performed.

What I really loved about that Celtics cap was its size – I have a very small head. This particular cap was a children's version. While my head size has not changed, I'm a bit taller now and as an adult, the children's brims are a tad too small. I often think about going back to them. Adult fitted caps start at 6⅞ if you're lucky enough to find one, and most of the cool caps in the Bronx or Harlem shops start at 7⅛. I tried upsizing when I had longer hair but it just didn't work for me – it would fly off in the slightest wind. I want function, not just to like the cap's look.

What does a person's cap tell you about their personality?

It's not as though you can tell things about someone's life through a cap straight off the bat, but I do want to know where the cap came from. For example, did the fella go to Harvard Business School, or did he buy his cap at the gift shop when he was visiting his son? Did he fight on some Navy ship or does he just love America, like I do? Recently, I saw a few older gentlemen wearing bicycle caps while strolling around Lincoln Center during Fashion Week, and asked, 'Why this cap?' It's always the same response, 'Oh, this? I've been wearing it for 20 years!' That's what I love about how a man wears his cap, hat or clothing. He owns it!

For me, growing up an orthodox Jew, it's very important to always have my head covered. I've almost never been photographed without a hat or cap and I don't recall ever leaving the house without some type of head covering. I feel naked with nothing over my head. Aside from religious upbringing or custom, I think men should wear hats or caps, as it's nice to remove your hat on entering a restaurant or someone's house, or when you greet a lady. I'm young-ish, but I'm traditional, and love the old-school days when men were gentlemen.

Is there a cap that you've always wanted but never obtained?

There are a few caps I've never been able to get in my size. Supreme made a Liberty London floral fitted this season, and even though their designer has the same size head as me, they don't make them that small. I've always wanted a few on-field caps like the Houston Astros and Montreal Expos and just never bought them.

A-RON

Former skater, model, clothing label owner and style maven Aaron Bondaroff (or A-Ron, as he likes to be called) knows a thing or two about caps. He is more often than not recognized for being the face of skate brand Supreme New York. After watching Supreme prosper, A-Ron decided to start up his own brand, launching his own label and opening a store called aNYthing (a New York thing). Since then, the label has established itself firmly in the streetwear market. A-Ron has worked on numerous caps and aNYthing and has now relocated to Los Angeles, where he is co-founder and director of the OHWOW gallery.

Caps are now a significant part of streetwear. When did your relationship with them begin?

I think caps are bigger than streetwear. I remember seeing baby pictures of myself wearing caps. The first caps I got into were snapbacks from my local baseball teams, like the New York Mets. A lot of people play Little League baseball at a young age and a cap is part of the uniform, so it is the first thing you wear that shows that you are a part of something. For me, that's where it all begins.

The cap has gone from being a functional item to an essential accessory. Why do you think that is?

People wear caps for many reasons. Some people wear the same cap because it's their lucky cap, or until it is dirty and beat-up. I remember when it came to the b-boy thing, you wanted to keep your cap clean and crispy, even to the point where the label tag was still on to emphasize how new it was. It also got to the point where your cap would coordinate with your clothes and sneakers. This started when I was in junior high. I didn't even care what team the cap was for as long as the colour matched my outfit. I remember always having caps; I remember getting my first fitted caps. I remember having Japanese baseball league caps. I always wanted caps that had a meaning and that nobody else had. I remember hanging all my caps on my bedroom wall above my bed from the ages of 10 to 15. It was like my first shot at merchandising.

Did you have any input on any of the designs at Supreme? If so, which was your favourite?

There have been so many through the years. I didn't have much input on designs. Supreme really put a stamp on the camp cap. I was lucky to put a new one on every day. I still wear Supreme caps; I've got one on today. I wish I had kept all of them. It's amazing how important that cap is in cap culture. It's almost like wearing a New York Yankees fitted. It shows you're part of something underground. Kids who can't afford Supreme clothing can buy the cap to get involved in the movement.

What has influenced the aNYthing brand?

I remember when hipsters were getting into Nike Dunks and trucker caps. The trucker cap is my favourite, the mesh back with the adjustment. It's the best looking, the best fitting, not that heavy on the head. So when I decided to make products, the trucker hat is what I wanted to use. I sort of wanted to make bootleg-looking items, so I used brands that I was involved in or interested in. Colt-45 was the 40-ounce of choice when I was drinking a lot of beer; Arm & Hammer was an ingredient in cooking up a certain drug. I was intrigued by street culture and drug references, as I was living a dirty lifestyle at the time. I wanted to turn it into a fashion thing.

Is there any hat you don't currently own that you'd like to have?

It's tough now because it's easier for people to make products. The smaller brands create something new but, sooner or later, the bigger brands will copy that and sell it on a larger scale, making that style of cap almost redundant in terms of originality. Ten to 15 years ago it was easier to find things that other people couldn't get, or alternative stuff. The Internet has changed that. But I recently got a Tower Records trucker cap from their store in Tokyo; the store in New York has closed down, so this cap was both nostalgic and cheap. For me, the cheaper the better!

Any other favourite caps?

I've been wearing caps for 30 years now, so it's hard to pick favourites. I've had so many; I go through phases. I remember when I was young wearing a Goofy cap with the big teeth and ears; I thought I looked cool.

Do you have a signature style when it comes to wearing caps?

I wear my snapback kind of big to make my head look small and also to hide my face. There's a certain type of way people wear their hats to feel comfortable or to add their own style, to own it. You can wear a cap traditional-style, but I like to throw in my attitude.

CRAIG FORD

Craig Ford's interest in streetwear dates back to the late 1980s. Now operating a successful showroom and brand agency, A Number of Names (or anon*), he manages brands such as Billionaire Boys Club/Ice Cream, Mr. Bathing Ape, Human Made, Bedwin & the Heartbreakers, Gourmet Footwear and aNYthing.

Can you remember your first cap?

When I was about 11 or 12 I was into breakdancing, but where I grew up in Scotland you couldn't get caps anywhere. I went abroad for the first time, on holiday to Majorca, and while I was there I bought a red, white and blue 6-panel cap with piping. When I went to go through customs on the way home, wearing the cap sideways, my dad made me take it off, as he said that I looked a mess and I was representing my country.

Can you tell me what the most popular style of cap is in terms of sales?

Our company distributes Ebbets Field Flannels, which mainly produces fitted caps, but we've started selling more strap and snapback caps from them. For Billionaire Boys Club it used to be all about New Era fitted, but there was a big rush on snapbacks last year and they still seem to be pretty popular.

What's your favourite cap?

The Ebbets anon* cap.

How does the cap represent A Number of Names?

It spells out our company name via 'a n o n *' characters spread across the panels. The asterisk is part of our branding and I thought it was interesting to use it, as you don't often see punctuation marks on caps. We have a strong graphic identity and we use a modern font which is not normally used on caps. I really liked that feature.

Why did you choose to make a cap with Ebbets Field?

They make the greatest quality baseball caps in the world. We distribute the brand and they are just really beautiful, handmade objects.

What's your favourite style of cap?

I like the wool fitted Ebbets. They look archetypally American to me. You can wear them with a button-down shirt and chinos and still look smart. I love the way older American men like Steve Reich wear them. When I had slightly longer hair at the back I once got compared to Arthur Russell, which I didn't mind, as he was a pretty smart guy.

Do you have a collection of caps?

I've had many caps over the years, but I've mostly given them away or got rid of them. When I was into punk I was into a kind of anarchy skate punk band from Darlington called Dan; they had an amazing cat logo. I got a hippie I knew to hand-paint it in fluorescent orange on a black snapback. I wish I still had that. I still have a few old ones; an old wool Stussy one, the hand-painted Supreme Rammellzee foam mesh, and an old BAPE flex fit with a version of the Nas logo. I now borrow a lot of Ebbets samples day to day.

Is there a cap that you always wanted but never obtained?

I always wanted the Big Audio Dynamite cap in cord. My mate had one and I borrowed it to go to their gig at the Glasgow Barrowlands when I was 16. I was down the front enjoying the gig when somebody swiped it off my head. I'd like to get one of those to wear now and one to give to my friend to replace his.

In the UK, do you think the type of person who wears a cap has changed over the years?

The way Americans wear caps is totally natural. The way a British man wears a flat cap or an 8-piece is part of his heritage, but when a British person wears a cap they are appropriating something from another culture; it's more of a statement. Now that the world is more homogenized, arguably Americanized, it's becoming less of a statement for somebody from the UK to wear a cap. The recent trend in menswear for all things rugged has also made it more acceptable to wear a cap in fashion circles and distanced it from the street look.

How important is the cap in today's street culture?

Caps have always been a part of street culture, from the early days of the b-boy to the present day, with fashion brands like Kenzo doing New Eras and Don C doing his thing. For a while it seemed as though every bedroom brand was knocking out pocket tees and 5-panel caps. They are ubiquitous.

BRIAN PROCELL

Brian Procell is a vintage clothing connoisseur from New York City. In 2006, he opened up a small store dedicated to vintage sportswear, including a large selection of headwear. It reintroduced New York to deadstock vintage sports caps from the 1980s and '90s. In 2008, he created a vintage sportswear consulting firm that offered services to a very elite group of local brands. In 2013, Procell opened a self-named shop on New York's Lower East Side that doubles as a showroom. Inside are offerings ranging from rare caps to outerwear and accessories – a true haven for vintage fans.

How long have you been wearing caps?

I didn't like beanies or knitted hats when I was a kid, so my mother would occasionally buy me caps to keep my head warm in the winter. I really became serious about wearing them when I was around 10. The pressure to wear your best to school and dress to impress really began to build up around that time. It seemed very instinctual and, since it was the early 1990s, sportswear fashion was becoming more of an integral part of the urban culture I was raised in. It seemed as though everyone started wearing baseball-style caps and they were all over the streets. I remember becoming obsessed with the embroidery on the caps I saw. The more information the hat communicated, the better it was in my eyes. Naturally, I gravitated toward the Starter brand of caps, which had a very distinct embroidered logo on the back of the crown. Their iconic style of branding really set them apart from other cap brands and they seemed to have every Major League licence under the sun. Prior to my Starter obsession, I had a small collection of black script LA Raiders hats that were sun-bleached and sweated out. They were made by Sports Specialties and were given to me by my older gang-banging half-brother; he grew up in South Central Los Angeles, where those particular hats were extremely popular.

Can you remember your first cap?

The first hat I ever owned was a BOY London hat, which my mother bought me in the late 1980s. She found it in a discount goods and overstock depot. It was a very simple black baseball cap with bold white letters that spelled out 'BOY'. My mother thought it was cute and I didn't really think much of it. But I really enjoyed the idea of wearing a hat, because no one else in my grade was wearing one. I felt as though it set me apart and I enjoyed the attention it brought me. I wore the hat every day on my commute to school until, one day, my Language Arts teacher looked at me and said 'Boy!? Is that so your parents don't get confused?' I responded by flicking him my middle finger.

What's your favourite type of cap?

I'm really into 5-panel camp caps and hats inspired by an outdoor sportsman lifestyle, such as long-bill fishing caps and mesh running caps. These are usually on heavy rotation in my personal mix, but I can't discount the classic appeal of the 1990s 6-panel baseball cap.

What makes a good cap?

Size and fit are always preoccupations when considering a cap, but that is subjective because heads come in every shape and size. To me, a good cap should always be made with attention to the quality of the materials. Manufacturers and designers should never cheap out on fabrics, hardware and other components, like the brim's armature and the closures.

Do you think caps are an important part of an outfit?

As important as any other part. They are so versatile, and can be either the ultimate understated complement or the main focal point of the outfit.

Which brand do you think produces the most interesting caps?

Supreme has the ability to produce variations of hats throughout the season. Also, the size of their collection overall is impressive. Kenzo's netted long-bill hat shows an interesting use of layering. Patrik Ervell caps are technical and outerwear-inspired.

What types of caps do you sell in your store?

The caps I currently offer are mostly from the 1990s. It's a very eclectic mix with an emphasis on American outdoor brands, such as Patagonia, Filson, Arc'teryx, The North Face and Columbia Sportswear. The collection also has representation from classic athletic brands like Nike and Adidas. Rare hats from Ralph Lauren are always in stock because of their strong New York cult following. I also like selecting hats from labels that are not usually associated with or known for producing caps, like Levi's, J. Crew, The Gap and Esprit. I enjoy rare and unusual design as well as a good backstory.

Where do you find your caps?

I can't give away all my secrets, but flea markets, thrift stores, estate sales and online auctions are some of the more conventional places I visit to procure my caps.

KISH PATEL

London-based Kish Patel is a world-renowned trainer collector who boasts a collection of around 3,000 pairs. However, footwear is not the only item he is enthusiastic about: records and headwear are also on his agenda, and he owns almost 400 caps. Kish has spent over 20 years witnessing the growth of cap culture in the UK and has expansive knowledge on the subject.

When did you start wearing caps?

Definitely in the 1980s. If you were into hip-hop you had to rock a baseball cap; it was an integral part of the look.

What caps did you wear back then?

The only brands that were available: labels like Starter, The Game, Sports Specialties and New Era. For me, fitteds were more special as they were size-specific and generally of higher quality, plus they were the on-field hat. I was rocking MLB caps but trying to find Minor League and college teams' caps to wear as well. Later, I moved on to teams that had folded, moved or changed name, such as the Brooklyn Dodgers, via the Cooperstown Collection. After that it was all about finding Negro League teams.

Slick Willies on High Street Kensington was a great spot to cop anything related to American sports; so was Mr USA in Wood Green Shopping Centre. Visiting relatives abroad was great, as you could go on the hunt – but trying to get New Era caps from teams not associated with where my relatives lived was hard, as distribution wasn't like it is now. Only the teams associated with the city you were in were available; it was tough to grab a Yankees hat in Houston, for example. Plus, you had to go to the team's stadium or arena.

Snapbacks were easier to get, as they were licenced products. I was always after Georgetown-related attire for some reason, maybe down to Dr Dre (from the hip-hop group Original Concept) rocking a Georgetown Starter jacket on the cover of an LP, or because of Patrick Ewing. My Georgetown Starter hats always got looks and comments; people wanted to know where I got them. Back then you never gave up your spots for anything, whether it was clothes, sneakers or even records.

What are your most prized possessions?

The cap samples that never went into production. I've got a Crooked Tongues New Era cap that C-Law designed which swapped the Oakland Raiders logo for a sandtrooper from *Star Wars*. It never came out.

Do you collect caps, or are they just part of your everyday attire?

They're just a part of my daily uniform. Sometimes I put a cap on that clashes with what I'm wearing. They're kind of like ties: you can wear them in many ways and they offer freedom of expression.

What's your favourite type of cap?

That's an easy one: it's definitely a fitted cap, as that's the original on-field version. Snapbacks are cool but were generally the cheaper, more accessible versions back in the day. The made-to-measure aspect of a fitted adds to the personal attachment to it, almost as if you had gone to Savile Row to purchase a suit.

KEVIN POON

Kevin Poon is an entrepreneur and fashion designer. Together with Edison Chen, he founded Hong Kong-based streetwear brand CLOT.

Can you remember your first cap?

I've been wearing caps for as long as I remember. My first cap was likely from Disneyland. The top part of the cap was Mickey Mouse's head. I think I was 6 years old. I definitely started appreciating caps in high school though. That was when I had a sense of what type of caps I liked to wear. It was an important aspect of my school wardrobe and I'd be always reppin' my favourite sport teams.

How many caps are in your collection?

I would say over 2,000. I started it a long time ago, which would explain the variety of caps I own. The headwear game is important. One cannot have too many shoes; it's the same with caps.

Where do you find your caps?

I don't go to special cap stores. Whatever I like is what I buy. I also get a lot of caps from friends as gifts.

Why do you wear a cap?

Caps are a great way to mix and match. Just like a T-shirt or footwear, a cap can really add something extra to make you feel your outfit is complete. How you wear your cap is very important. I like to wear a New Era hat with a simple T-shirt, jeans and a pair of Jordans. I really don't think it's some sort of science … wear whatever you like and be confident about it.

What's your favourite style of cap?

Lately, it's the snapback. It's simple and easy to rock. It fits comfortably, is adjustable to how you want to wear it and can easily be matched with your outfit. There are so many different colour schemes for snapbacks that they are easy to mix and match, especially when you collect them, like I do. Snapbacks are just so versatile in design. In my opinion, snapbacks are never a trend, but always in style.

Is there a big cap culture in Hong Kong?

Definitely not as big as in the States, because we don't have any renowned sports teams here, I feel. People love to rep their team, especially when they are from that city. There also aren't that many shops that sell a wide variety of caps. Most of the hottest and most popular caps come from overseas; they are brought in and sold at twice the normal price in local boutiques. I don't see that many people wearing them around, as I do in the States. Streetwear in Hong Kong is still growing and following other trends.

How many caps have CLOT produced, and which is your favourite?

To be honest, I don't know! Over 50 styles? The CLOT Royale x New Era were dope. The ones we did with SSUR recently for the Gutter Store are definitely noteworthy and so is the Fighting Bear New Era hat we released for Spring/ Summer 2013. It is RZA approved. He rocked it at Coachella on stage during the Wu-Tang reunion.

In your opinion, who produces the best caps?

New Era has always set the benchmark for quality caps for streetwear. Larose also make high-quality panel caps that I am a big fan of.

Why do you think the cap is an important part of street culture and streetwear?

As I said, it completes the wardrobe. Sport is also a big part of street culture and streetwear. They go hand in hand. Streetwear is about making a statement, not necessarily a fashion statement, more like an opinion. If you like the Bulls, you'll most likely have a Bulls cap. If you want people to fuck off, you'll probably have a hat that says something along those lines. That's the way it goes in streetwear …

Is there any cap that you never had that you would like to get your hands on?

I don't recall. There are so many different ones coming out all the time that you soon forget the cap you loved last week.

UNCLE T

Christophe Lacroix, aka Uncle T or Tex, has been involved in the urban/hip-hop scene since the mid-1980s, beginning with graffiti and dance. He founded the first French hip-hop magazine, fanzine *Get Busy*, in 1990. He's also the co-founder of 360 Marketing and Promotion with Thibaut de Longeville, after a detour to New York with the music label Loud Records. Since then he has built 4x4 Marketing with DJ Cut Killer, and is currently the head of marketing at Wrung. Besides his marketing activities, he's a well-known DJ in Paris, releasing mixtapes under his alias Uncle T and hosting the party Groove Deluxe. Tex is an avid collector and connoisseur of sneakers, caps and Ralph Lauren vintage clothing.

How did you come across the cap?

I would say through hip-hop. Honestly, before 1983–4 and the rise of hip-hop in Paris and in France, you almost never saw anybody wearing a cap. Through the 1980s, if you wore a cap, that meant you were part of the hip-hop scene and came from *la banlieue* (the suburbs, or estates).

How popular is cap culture in Paris?

Right now cap culture is big in Paris. From people in their 40s to young teenagers, everybody wears a cap. There's not one structured scene, but many. Hip-hop fans, sneaker-heads, hipsters, skaters – each have their own specific scenes.

Where did it begin?

Everything begins in *la banlieue*!

What's your favourite cap?

A classic New York Yankees fitted style. Like the Nike Air Force 1 white-on-white shoe, it never goes out of style. And it goes with a lot of outfits I wear.

Who makes the best caps?

New Era for a fitted cap, Starter for the snapback, Ralph Lauren Polo for 5-panels and long-bills.

You are part of the Paris Lo-Life crew, made up of Polo by Ralph Lauren fanatics. How many of the brand's caps do you have?

Yes, I'm part of the Paris Polo Club! I have around 60 Ralph Lauren caps: fitted, long-bill and 5-panel styles.

What's the attraction of the Ralph Lauren caps?

The thing that interests me about them is that Ralph Lauren is always producing great colours and logos. It's easy to match the cap with an item of Ralph Lauren clothing; by doing that you can really create a sharp outfit.

MARIA FALBO

Maria Falbo is a skateboarder who runs the COPSON STREET blog, which she started while still a student in Manchester. Now based in London, Maria has diversified the COPSON brand, establishing a T-shirt line and COPSON Creative Studio.

Do you remember your first cap?

It was an Altamont trucker hat. I have been through all the phases of headwear, from bandanas to visors, truckers, New Eras, etc.

How long have you been wearing caps?

I think I've been rocking them since I was around 14. Definitely started at puberty. I own over 50 of them.

What's your favourite type of cap?

A classic snapback.

Who do you think makes the best caps?

It's all about the deadstock NFL caps. Nowadays Huf make some good ones.

Is there a cap you've always wanted that you never had?

It'll be some random one-off 1980s merch cap. They always seem to be the best. I have one from JCB that is the perfect example: it's an all-over tropical print snapback. So random but so good. Another is my mum's Hotel Atlantis merchandise hat from a trip to the Bahamas. Winner.

Do you think you can tell a lot about a person by the cap they wear?

Nowadays I'm not sure you can. Hats have become so hyped, people may just be wearing them because they saw them in *GQ* or *Grazia* magazine.

Over the years more females have started to wear caps: why do you think that is?

It's definitely a massive trend at the moment. Like trainers, hats have become more mainstream and appear in fashion magazines. In a way it's annoying, but it also means that wearing a cap on any occasion is more acceptable, which I'm grateful for.

Do you think females who wear caps are still stereotyped as tomboys?

Absolutely not. It has become a mainstream trend now for girls to wear caps. Every high-street retailer seems to have caps in their collections. It's the same with trainers. Somehow the tomboy image seems to have influenced women's trends massively.

You're a skateboarder; do you think this has influenced your style?

Absolutely. I think being a skateboarder shapes your style and attitude towards life. Even though I am a skateboarder, I don't always dress like one, but I think there are always slight influences of skate style in there.

Where do you find your caps? Do you have a favourite store?

My favourites are often one-off deadstock caps. They are unique, so you won't be wearing what everyone else has got on. I recently got a great one from Polar Skate Co. eBay is my go-to place, I guess.

Do you have any style icons?

Alex from *Flashdance* and Tony Montana from *Scarface*.

Do you envision designing caps for the COPSON STREET brand? If so, who would you like to collaborate with?

Absolutely! It is on the agenda: I'm just waiting for the perfect idea. It would be great to work with Starter on something classic.

What skateboarder's style do you like?

Brent Atchley – for the blissful nonchalance in his skate style and his look. He always wraps his mane under a cap.

relective silver (
--inspired by ch
--dot print uses

front panel: thi

body fabric: 4-(

shape: nike SB

back strap: san

JON TAGUCHI

Jon Taguchi resides in Portland, Oregon, and designs headwear. In 1986, Jon got his first break in the apparel industry, designing accessories for Esprit International in San Francisco. During the early 1990s, Jon relocated north to Nike's headquarters in Portland. There he took on the role of Senior Designer of Headwear. During his period at Nike, Jon worked on several iconic running caps.

What factors do you need to take into account when designing
a running cap?

I found that runners, along with cyclists, are extremely discerning and picky about the smallest of details. Shaving a few grams of weight off a product is a big deal. Re-engineering a seam or eliminating one in just the right way can make the difference between a good product and a great one that the consumer will love and personally connect with. The innovations are always in the service of performance — the functionality of being lightweight, breathable, ventilated, wicking, reflective, comfortable, secure, adjustable and so on.

Regarding production, have you discovered or invented any new
technologies?

At Nike the big ideas were incubated and rolled out seasonally for all designers by various advance design/trend teams. A great designer, like a great chef, does not invent so much as synthesize tried and true techniques and materials in a subtly new way that brings delight — or other more tangible benefits. That said, I was awarded 4 utility patents and a couple of design patents during my tenure at Nike.

What type of testing process do you have?

We wear-test our caps on real athletes.

How many caps have you designed?

A lot! Well over 100 unique styles per year, for many years. For every design that was mass-produced, there were 3 or 4 or even 12 more designs that didn't make it.

Out of all the caps you have designed, do you have a favourite?

The Tailwind from 2003. We innovated the inside construction by replacing the sweatband inside with an integrated sweat 'panel'. That really did well for us. But I am most proud of the Dri-FIT Featherlight, which was produced in 100 per cent regenerated virgin-quality polyester.

Do you wear caps?

I've worn and loved almost every type of hat imaginable. I used to change hats every couple of hours at work, so anyone who saw me throughout the day would see me in a different hat each time I came by. My favourite right now is a black, grey and white knit fedora by Ben Sherman.

What type of caps do you see us wearing in the future?

Everything simply cycles around and comes back again. Trend forecasters keep telling us that UV protection will be increasingly important. I also believe that wearable technology should integrate into headwear, as it already has in eyewear and wristwatches.

VICTOR OSORIO

Victor Osorio is a Senior Design Manager at Mitchell & Ness Nostalgia Co. in Philadelphia. He's been involved in the licenced cap business since 1993, beginning his career with a company called Signature Sportswear. In 1995, he relocated to Twins New York, where he became a designer. In 2003, he worked for Reebok and then moved on to Adidas in 2006, where he established a range of fitted and on-court caps. In 2008, he joined Mitchell & Ness, where, in the autumn of 2008, he added the first snapback style to their seasonal collection. By 2009, snapback sales had exploded for the company.

How did you get started in the industry?

I was fortunate enough to win second prize in a Design Your Own Cap contest held by Signature Sportswear back in 1993, at the High School of Art & Design in New York City. When I claimed my prize, I was offered a summer job as a production artist. I worked on production art for a couple of years until 1996, when I developed into a full-time designer for Twins New York, now known as '47 Brand. It's been an amazing journey that I credit to perseverance, positive energy and good business skills.

What approach do you take when designing a cap?

It depends on the project or the client. For Mitchell & Ness, my number 1 approach is drawing inspiration from sports history – any sports history. The stories behind a certain player, jersey or period are what really get me going. Mix that with my graffiti and hip-hop music upbringing and you get a massive pool of inspiration.

How long does it take to turn your initial designs into the finished caps we see in stores?

It all depends on the level of the project. A quick project can be turned around in 45 to 60 days, from initial design to selling the cap in-store. The average time for a planned out inline collection is anywhere from 4 to 5 months.

Do you have a favourite cap you've worked on?

It's too hard to pick just one. As far as standouts in my career go, I have say the Kolors Collection for Reebok, the Ligature Series for Adidas NBA, Mitchell & Ness player or team commemorative caps, Mitchell & Ness Special Script styles and collaborations with good brands, boutiques or creative individuals.

Do you collect caps?

Yes indeed. Growing up, the local video store in my neighbourhood sold snapbacks in the back for $10, so that sparked everything. They carried The Game, Starter, Logo7 and Signature, to name a few. Today, my collection consists of primarily sport-licenced fitted and snapback caps with a few other hat silhouettes sprinkled in.

In today's market, why do you think caps are so important?

Whether it's sports or fashion, your uniform is not complete without a good cap to top it off. It's the definitive piece of your style or affiliation.

The Fresh Prince of Bel-Air's 5-panel

NBC's *The Fresh Prince of Bel Air*, starring Will Smith, was a hugely popular sitcom during the 1990s, and remains an important part of American television history to this day. Throughout the course of the show, Smith wore a wide variety of caps and hats. However, this mysterious 5-panel is the most iconic.

CAPS MADE FAMOUS

Like a chameleon, the cap can blend into almost any surroundings: it has starred in classic films and commercials, been worn by winners on podiums and occasionally shielded notorious criminals from the prying lenses of photographers. If you look for them, you can see that caps have played a part in images of iconic moments in both popular culture and sport throughout modern history. Sometimes we can only appreciate fashions in hindsight, but now that celebrity attire is scrutinized like never before, caps have stepped into the limelight. They have become the recognized trademarks of our favourite thrash metal or hip-hop groups, and been used to make statements in many seminal music videos. Our heroes – whether athletes, actors, rappers or rockers – all wear caps.

Tri-Mountain Baseball Club

Tri-Mountain was the first club in New England to leave behind 'round ball', also known as 'the Massachusetts game' (the region's traditional version of baseball), in order to adopt the New York version initiated by the Knickerbocker Baseball Club. The Tri-Mounts helped to ensure that by the end of the Civil War, teams far and wide played the New York game – the version of baseball most people play today.

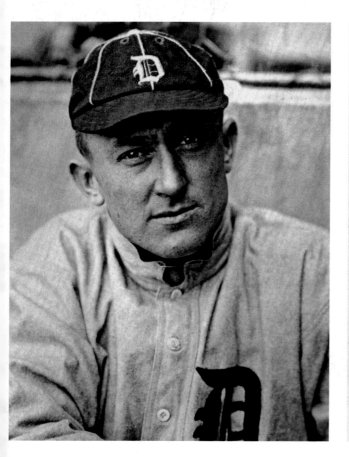

<u>Ty Cobb</u>

Ty Cobb is widely recognized for setting 90 MLB records during his career, many of which he still holds. In 1994, a biographical movie of his life, *Cobb*, was released; it starred Tommy Lee Jones.

<u>Vintage Cigarette Card</u>

By early 1886, images of baseball players were often featured on cards that came in American cigarette packets. These were included partly for promotional purposes and partly because the card helped protect the cigarettes from damage. This vintage cigarette card from Allen & Ginter features an illustration of Adrian 'Cap' Anson, who is regarded by historians as having had a key role in establishing the racial segregation in baseball that persisted until the late 1940s.

Chinese Soldiers' Long-Bill Caps

In the late 1940s, some Chinese Nationalist soldiers wore long-bill fitted caps made from cotton while working. These protected their eyes from the sun and acted as additional padding for their helmets.

Joseph Plunkett Youth Organization Cap

Joseph Plunkett was a Democratic ward boss from Chicago who organized free events for delinquent children in the 1940s. Those who attended would leave with a bag of candy bars, a comic book and sometimes a cap. The bag and cap would have 'Joe Plunkett Youth' printed on them – a great example of using a cap as a promotional item.

Willie Stargell's Pittsburgh Pirates Pillbox

The late Wilver Dornell 'Willie' Stargell, nicknamed 'Pops', wears his special Pittsburgh Steelers pillbox cap at a 1962 game. The crown was covered in embroidered stars. Rumour has it that players would receive a star from Stargell for good performances. These soon became known as Stargell stars.

Jackie Robinson's Brooklyn Dodgers Cap

Jack Roosevelt 'Jackie' Robinson was the first African American to play MLB. He helped guide the Brooklyn Dodgers to 6 pennants and a World Series Championship. Some now consider his Brooklyn Dodgers number 42 shirt and matching 'B' cap to be symbols of courage.

Cycling Caps

Jacques Anquetil, Eddie Merckx and Felice Gimondi are 3 cycling legends whose names are hugely respected in the international cycling community. These cycling caps from the 1970s are still worn today, since fans adore their traditional designs. These riders were sponsored by an array of brands: Anquetil by BIC Biro, Merckx by Peugeot and Gimondi by Salvarani.

The Beastie Boys' Trucker Caps

At a time when most hip-hop artists were flamboyant, the Beastie Boys went
in the opposite direction. Their on- and off-stage appearance was the same.
Here they are pictured wearing promotional trucker caps.

Dorothy 'Tootie' Ramsey's Baseball Cap

Actress Kim Fields played the part of Dorothy 'Tootie' Ramsey on the 1980s American sitcom *The Facts of Life*. The charismatic Tootie managed the school's baseball team with unconventional methods.

Arthur Scargill's United Mine Workers of America Cap

Arthur Scargill was the president of the UK's National Union of Mineworkers from 1982 until 2002, and led the union through the 1984 miners' strike. Here, Scargill is seen wearing a UMWA (United Mine Workers of America) cap. The UMWA is an American labour union best known for representing coal miners and coal technicians.

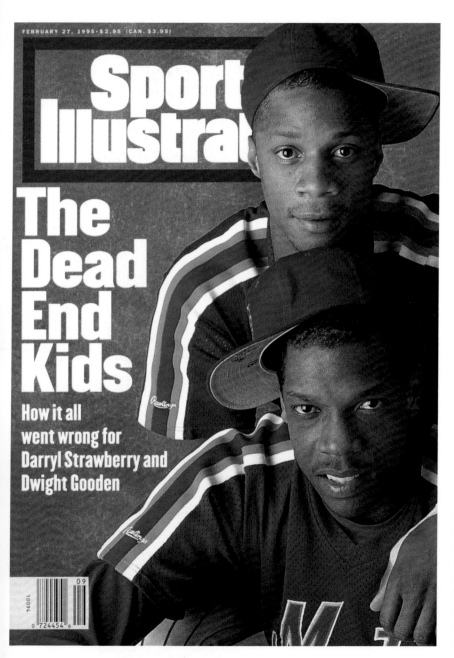

Darryl Strawberry and Dwight Gooden's Mets Caps

Darryl Strawberry and Dwight Gooden played for the New York Mets, and were popular characters due to their on- and off-pitch antics. Both players had controversial relationships with drugs and alcohol. However, their awards and achievements in the game are still highly regarded. In 1995 *Sports Illustrated* published an image of the pair on its cover wearing their Mets caps in an unorthodox sideways fashion.

Keith Haring's BMX Cap

Pop artist Keith Haring was often seen wearing caps. Here he is in Tokyo in the late 1980s, wearing a BMX-inspired cycling cap.

Spike Lee and Flava Flav's 40 Acres and a Mule and Public Enemy Bullseye Caps

Film director Spike Lee is rarely seen without a cap. He founded his production company, 40 Acres and a Mule Filmworks, in the late 1980s, and has since parlayed it into a clothing brand. Rap group Public Enemy's Flava Flav wears a cap that includes the group's iconic bullseye logo.

CAPS ON FILM

Caps have frequently featured in movies. Often they are an important part of a character's costume, adding depth to their persona or visually expressing part of the story. A few caps have been created just for the movies they feature in, while others were made famous by the characters who wore them, and some are common designs that add a note of authenticity.

Back to the Future Part II, 1989 (above)

The main character, Marty McFly, dons a full iridescent baseball cap supposed to represent the style of cap we will all be wearing in 2015.

Boyz n the Hood, 1991

In this film the character Doughboy, played by rapper Ice Cube, wears a Detroit Tigers baseball cap. After the release of the movie, the team's 'D' logo became associated with the Doughboy character.

Indiana Jones and the Temple of Doom, 1984

Short Round from _Indiana Jones_ wears a short-bill New York Mets baseball cap.

Forrest Gump, 1994

Forrest Gump, played by Tom Hanks, honours his good friend Bubba by wearing his Bubba Gump

Wayne's World, 1992

Comedian Mike Myers created this classic comedy film, which starred characters that first appeared on the TV show _Saturday Night Live_. The 'Wayne's World' promotional cap was worn by the character throughout his appearances on television and in movies.

Ed, 1996

Matt LeBlanc stars as a player for Minor League Baseball team the Santa Rosa Rockets. The team mascot, a chimpanzee, wears the same cap as him. This may be the only time an animal has worn a baseball cap on film.

The Comrades of Summer, 1992 (above)

This made-for-TV movie featured a Russian Olympic baseball team managed by an ex-Major League Baseball team.

The Fan, 1996 (below)

The baseball fanatic played by Robert De Niro wears the cap of his beloved baseball team, the San Francisco Giants. The cap is a visual representation of his obsession for the baseball player Bobby Rayburn, played by Wesley Snipes.

Major League, 1989

The Cleveland Indians was the team of choice for this movie. Charlie Sheen played the character Vaughn, nicknamed 'Wild Thing'.

Janet Jackson's 1814 Cap

Recording artist Janet Jackson released her *Rhythm Nation 1814* album in 1989, along with an early military-inspired promotional video. In the video, Janet wears a cap with a metal '1814' emblem; the significance of the number is that R (for rhythm) is the 18th letter in the alphabet, and N (for nation) is the 14th. Janet also wore this on the album's cover.

<u>Andre Agassi's Nike Cap</u>

<u>Michael Jordan's 1991 Chicago Bulls Championship Winners Snapback</u>

Sponsorship is a big deal in the game of tennis. However, both tennis branding and the general appearance of players were once quite reserved. When the champion Andre Agassi first came to prominence in the 1990s, his appearance was far from subtle; in fact, his whole style screamed 'anti-establishment'. During certain matches, Agassi wore a cap to hide his flowing locks of hair.

Here, former NBA superstar Michael Jordan wears a 1991 Chicago Bulls Championship Winners snapback. At the end of every Championship playoff game, the winning team receives a cap noting their accomplishments. Over the years these winning caps have been manufactured by various brands, and replicas are collector's items.

Bill Clinton's Duck-Hunting Cap

In 1993, former United States President Bill Clinton exchanged his suit for duck-hunting attire. He is pictured here wearing a duck camouflage cap. At the time, this print was the pattern of choice for a large assortment of menswear.

Jay-Z's Yankees Cap

Rapper and record producer Jay-Z has sported a New York Yankees cap for many years. He's worn it on album covers and in music videos, and has helped turn it into a universal icon. No matter what part of the world you visit, you can always find a Yankees cap for sale. As Jay-Z says in his song 'Empire State of Mind', he's made the cap more famous than the Yankees themselves.

Wiley's Nike Cap

In the early 2000s, Nike running caps were widespread in Europe. The appearance of the UK-based recording artist Wiley reflected the style of British inner-city youth at that time.

Fred Durst's Red Yankees Cap

Fred Durst of Limp Bizkit sports a red New York Yankees cap. He wore the same style in 2004 in the video for 'Rollin' (Air Raid Vehicle)', in which guest star Ben Stiller refers to him as 'red cap'. This sealed the association of that cap with Durst and many Limp Bizkit fans purchased it in homage to their beloved front man.

Britney Spears' Ed Hardy Cap

In 2004, the French fashion designer Christian Audigier approached Ed Hardy, a tattoo artist, about using his work on a clothing line. Audigier could see the potential in Hardy's style of artwork and thought it would do well in the fashion world. A deal was struck, and Ed Hardy clothing was born. It did not take long for the brand to hit the mainstream, and celebrities such as Britney Spears were occasionally seen wearing Ed Hardy apparel.

Travis Barker's Dave's Quality Meat x New Era Cap

The American musician, producer and entrepreneur Travis Barker is rarely seen without a cap. In 2008, he wore a limited-edition Dave's Quality Meat x New Era cap that he had produced with New Era as part of their 'Capture the Flag' collection.

Pharrell Williams' N*E*R*D* Cap

During the early 2000s, Pharrell Williams was widely known for his yellow trucker cap emblazoned with the name of his band, N*E*R*D (or Nobody Ever Really Dies). This encouraged a huge wave of fans to sport trucker caps. Williams isn't solely responsible for the resurrection of the trucker cap, but he did expose it to a wider audience.

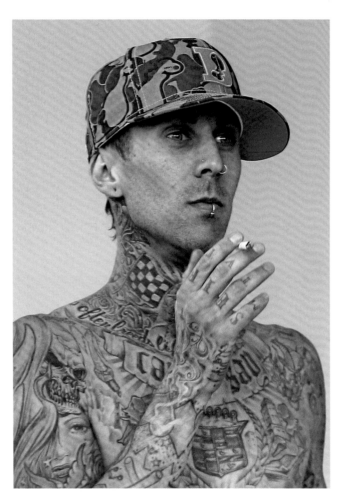

9/11 Memorial Cap

This cap was hung on the fence at Ground Zero as a mark of respect for those who lost their lives in the attacks on the World Trade Center in New York. The words 'Rest in peace, see you in heaven' have been written on the brim.

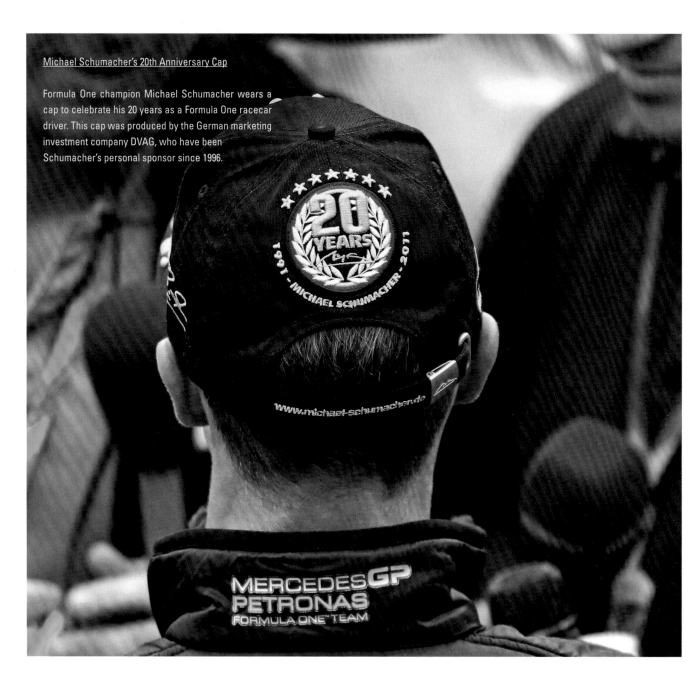

Michael Schumacher's 20th Anniversary Cap

Formula One champion Michael Schumacher wears a
cap to celebrate his 20 years as a Formula One racecar
driver. This cap was produced by the German marketing
investment company DVAG, who have been
Schumacher's personal sponsor since 1996.

Lewis Hamilton's Formula One Cap

In 2008, Lewis Hamilton became the youngest driver ever to win the Formula One World Championship. The cap he wore on the podium has become a collector's item.

<u>Tyler the Creator's Supreme Camp Cap</u>

In 2011, Tyler the Creator, of Los Angeles-based hip-hop collective Odd Future, picked up an MTV Award for Best New Artist. Tyler wore a corduroy leopard-brimmed Supreme cap, one of the most sought-after caps that season.

<u>Rihanna's Kenzo x New Era Cap</u>

Def Jam recording artist Rihanna is often photographed sporting a cap. On this occasion, she was spotted wearing a Kenzo x New Era cap from 2012.

A$AP Rocky's Black Scale Cap

In 2012, A$AP Rocky erupted into the hip-hop spotlight; his style and charisma awarded him with huge amounts of attention. Rocky's profile exposed fans to clothing labels that had previously been unnoticed by the hip-hop community, such as Alexander Wang and Raf Simons. San Francisco-based Black Scale is one of the brands Rocky wore frequently at the start of his career. To acknowledge him, Black Scale produced this 'VSVP' cap for Rocky.

Cap street style in New York.

STREET SNAPS

There's no single way to wear a cap. It can be sported by people on a quest to look their best, or those who are deliberately dressing down. Caps are worn by all types of people around the globe, and the only rule is to pair them with plenty of attitude.

NEW YORK

CAPS: ONE SIZE FITS ALL

LOS ANGELES

CAPS: ONE SIZE FITS ALL

CAPS: ONE SIZE FITS ALL

PARIS

CAPS: ONE SIZE FITS ALL

BERLIN

CAPS: ONE SIZE FITS ALL

SYDNEY

CAPS: ONE SIZE FITS ALL

SHOP INDEX

Houston

Urban Zone
4440 North Freeway
Houston, TX 77022
urbanzone.com

Las Vegas

Fruition Las Vegas
4139 South Maryland Parkway
Las Vegas, NV 89119
fruitionlv.com

KNYEW
3999 Spring Mountain Road
Las Vegas, NV 89102
knyew.com

Stussy
4480 Paradise Road
Suite 350
Las Vegas, NV 89109
stussy.com

Los Angeles

alife LA
1520 North Cahuenga
Suite 2
Los Angeles, CA 90028
rivingtonclub.com

American Rag
150 South La Brea Avenue
Los Angeles, CA 90036
amrag.com

Crooks & Castles
8021 Melrose Ave
Los Angeles, CA 90046
crooksncastles.com

Supreme
439 North Fairfax Ave
Los Angeles, CA 90036
supremenewyork.com

Undefeated LA
112.5 South La Brea Avenue
Los Angeles, CA 90036
undefeated.com

New York

Dave's Quality Meat
7 East 3rd Street
New York, NY 10003
dqmnewyork.com

Flight Club New York
812 Broadway
New York, NY 10003
flightclubny.com

Hat Club
103 Mercer Street
New York, NY 10012
hatclub.com

Memes NYC
3 Great Jones Street
New York, NY 10012
memes-nyc.com

New Era
9 East 4th Street
New York, NY 10003
neweracap.com

Reed Space
151 Orchard Street
New York, NY 10002
thereedspace.com

Supreme
274 Lafayette Street
New York, NY 10012
supremenewyork.com

Philadelphia

Mitchell & Ness Nostalgia Co.
1201 Chestnut Street
Philadelphia, PA 19107
mitchellandness.com

San Francisco

Fully Laced
Stonestown Galleria
577 Buckingham Way
San Francisco, CA 94132
fullylaced.com

Infinite SF
627 Post Street
San Francisco, CA 94109
infinitesf.com

Seattle

Ebbets Field Flannels
408 Occidental Avenue South
Seattle, WA 98104
ebbets.com

Washington, DC

Commonwealth
1781 Florida Avenue North West
Washington, DC, 20009
cmonwealth.com

Canada

Edmonton

Haven
10528 – 108 Street North West
Edmonton, AB T5H 2Z9
havenshop.ca

Toronto

Livestock
116 Spadina Avenue
Toronto, ON M5V 2K6
deadstock.ca

New Era
202 Queen Street West
Toronto, ON M5V 1Z9
neweracap.com

Snapback and Goods
786 St Clair Avenue West
Toronto, ON M6C 1B6
snapbackandgoods.com

Costa Rica

San José

Okapee
Callejón Dorado
Escazú, San José
okapeestore.wordpress.com

Mexico City

180°
Colima 180
Roma Norte
Mexico City 06700
180grados.mx

CommonPeople
Emilio Castelar 149
Colima Polanco
Mexico City 11560
commonpeople.com.mx

.DESTRUCTIBLE.
Colima 244
Roma Norte
Mexico City 06700
facebook.com/pages/DESTRUC-
TIBLE/45506814684

Headquarter
Colima 244
Planta Alta
Colima Roma
Mexico City 06700
headquarterstore.com

Argentina

Buenos Aires

Six Feet
Gurruchaga 1285
Buenos Aires
sixfeet.com.ar

Brazil

Rio de Janeiro

HomeGrown
Rua Maria Quitéria 68
Ipanema
Rio de Janeiro
homegrownrio.blogspot.co.uk

São Paulo

Guadalupe Store
Rua Três Rios, 126-Bom Retiro
01123-000 São Paulo
facebook.com/guadalupestoresp

Visionare
Rua Augusta 290
01304-000 São Paulo
visionairestore.com.br

United Kingdom

Aberdeen

Hanon
154 Market Street
Aberdeen AB11 5PP
hanon-shop.com

Bristol

5 pointz
18 Nelson Street
Bristol BS1 2LE
5pointz.co.uk

Donuts
8 Perry Road
Bristol BS1 5BQ
donutsthestore.co.uk

Edinburgh

Focus
270 Canongate
The Royal Mile
Edinburgh EH8 8AA
focuspocus.co.uk

Route One
29 Cockburn Street
Edinburgh EH1 1BN
routeone.co.uk

Glasgow

Aspecto
18–20 West Nile Street
Glasgow G1 2PW
aspecto.co.uk

Fat Buddha
73 St Vincent Street,
Glasgow G2 5TF
fatbuddhastore.com

London

BAPE London
4 Upper James St
London W1F 9DG
bape.com

The Candy Store
26 Berwick Street
London W1F 8RG
thecandystoreclothing.com

Garbstore
188 Kensington Park Road
London W11 2ES
couvertureandthegarbstore.com

The Goodhood Store
41 Coronet Street
London N1 6HD
goodhoodstore.com

The Hideout
7 Upper James Street
London W1F 9DH
hideoutstore.com

New Era
72–74 Brewer Street
London W1F 9JG
neweracap.co.uk

Present London
140 Shoreditch High Street
London E1 6JE
present-london.com

Slam City Skates
16 Neal's Yard
London WC2H 9DP
slamcity.com

Supreme
2/3 Peter Street
London W1F 0AA
supremenewyork.com

Trapstar
281 Portobello Road
Unit 21 Portobello Green Arcade
London W10 5TZ
iamatrapstar.com

Manchester

Oi Polloi
63 Thomas Street
Manchester M4 1LQ
oipolloi.com

Newcastle

End Clothing
4–6 High Bridge
Newcastle Upon Tyne NE1 1EN
endclothing.co.uk

Europe

Amsterdam

Patta
Zeedijk 67
1012 AS Amsterdam
patta.nl

Antwerp

Fish & Chips
Kammenstraat 36
Antwerp B-2000
fishandchips.be

Ben G
Nieuwezijds Voorburgwal 142
1012 SH Amsterdam
ben-g.nl

Barcelona

24 Kilates
Carrer del Comerç 29
Barcelona 08003
24-kts.com

Trust Nobody
C/ Tallers 1
Barcelona 08001
trustnobody.es

Berlin

ABOVE
Kastanienallee 87
10435 Berlin
above-berlin.de

Firmament
Linienstrasse 40
10119 Berlin
firmamentberlin.com

Soto
Torstrasse 72
10119 Berlin
sotostore.com

Treasures of the 90s
Innstrasse 42
12045 Berlin
treasuresofthe90s.com

Copenhagen

Norse Store
Pilestræde 41
1112 Copenhagen
norsestore.com

Wood Wood VII
Grønnegade 1
1107 Copenhagen
woodwood.dk

Madrid

Stussy
Calle de Argensola 10
Madrid 28004
stussy.com

Milan

Special Milano
Corso di Porta Ticinese 80
Milano 20127
specialmilano.com

Slam Jam Milan
Via Pasquale Paoli 3
20143 Milano
slamjamsocialism.com

Wok Store
Viale Col di Lana 5a
20136 Milano
wok-store.com

Paris

AUGUSTE
10 Rue Saint Sabin
75011 Paris
augusteparis.com

blackrainbow
68 Rue des Archives
75003 Paris
blackrainbow-shop.com/fr

Citadium
33 Rue Quincampoix
75004 Paris
citadium.com

colette
213 Rue Saint-Honoré
75001 Paris
colette.fr

Pigalle
7 Rue Henry Monnier
75009 Paris
pigalleparis.fr

Stuttgart

SUPPA
Paulinenstrasse 44
70178 Stuttgart
suppastore.com

Russia

Moscow

Fott
Dmitrov lane 7
107031 Moscow
shop.fott.ru

South Africa

Cape Town

Baseline Studio
162 Long Str
Cape Town 8000
baselinestudio.co.za

Loading Bay
30 Hudson Street
De Waterkant
Cape Town 8001
loadingbay.co.za

Shelflife
119 Loop Street
Cape Town 8001
shelflife.co.za

Smith & Abrahams
103 Sir Lowry Road
Cape Town 7925
smithandabrahams.co.za

Unknown Union
24 Kloof Street
Cape Town 8008
unknownunion.co.za

Asia

Bangkok

Genesis
1st floor 1B41 MBK Center
Phayathai Road
Wangmai Pathumwan
Bangkok 10330
genesis-bkk.com

Outcast Store
236/11 Room No. 3, Siam Square Soi. 2
Rama 1 Road, Phatumwan
Bangkok 10330
outcaststorebkk.com

Sneaka Villa
226/7 Siam Square Soi 2
Rama 1 Road
Phatumwan
Bangkok 10330
sneakavilla.net

Beijing

BAPE
NLG-49
Village North Beijing
bape.com

HOODS
NLG 21–22
Village North Beijing
neighborhood.jp

Mess Beijing
484a Dong Si North Avenue
Dongcheng District
Beijing
messbeijing.com

Hong Kong

F.I.L. by Visvim
8–9 Sun Street
Hong Kong
visvim.tv

JUICE Hong Kong
9–11 Cleveland Street
Fashion Walk
Causeway Bay
Hong Kong
clotinc.com/retail

Y-3 – Hong Kong
18 Hanoi Road
K11 Art Mall Shop
Hong Kong G07-09-18
adidas.com/y-3

Jakarta

Otoko
Jalan Cipete Raya 55H
12410 Jakarta
otokostore.com

Penny
Jalan Bangka Raya 107
12720 Jakarta Selatan
penny-613.com

Kuala Lumpur

Crossover Concept Store
F1-66, Sunway Pyramid Shopping Mall
No. 3, Jalan PJS 11/15
Bandar Sunway
46150 Petaling Jaya
Selangor, Kuala Lumpur
crossoverconceptstore.blogspot.
co.uk

Hundred%
G50–51 and G66
Berjaya Times Square
55100 Kuala Lumpur
facebook.com/seratuspercent

JUICE KL
46 and 46–1, Jalan Telawi 5
Bangsar Baru
Kuala Lumpur
clotinc.com/retail

Pattern Store
55 Jalan SS15/4B,
Subang Jaya
Selangor
47500 Kuala Lumpur
instagram.com/patternstore

Stussy Chapter: KL
10 Jalan 1/77A, Pudu (behind Times
Square)
55100 Kuala Lumpur
stussy.com

Seoul

Addicted
634–11 1F Sinsadong
Seoul, Apgujeong
addicted.kr

Brown Breath
340–13 Seokyo-dong
Mapo-gu
Seoul, Hongdae Neighborhood
brownbreath.com

Daily Projects
1–24 Cheongdam-dong
Seoul, Cheongdam
dailyprojects.kr

Sculp
B1, 408–24, Seogyo-Dong
Mapo-Gu
Seoul
sculp.co.kr

Shanghai

JUICE Shanghai
832 Ju Lu Road
Shanghai 200040
clotinc.com/retail

Singapore

Know It Nothing
51 Haji Lane
Singapore 189244
knowitnothing.com

SURRENDER
Raffles Hotel Arcade
#02-31, 328 North Bridge Road
Singapore 188719
surrebderous.com

Taipei

JUICE Taipei
38 Lane 161, Section 1
Dunhua South Road
Da'an District
Taipei
clotinc.com/retail

Tokyo

alife Tokyo
3-15-10 Jingumae
Tokyo
alifenewyork.com

Blackflag
5-4-24-1F Minamiaoyama
Minato-ku
Tokyo
wtaps.com

BAPE Exclusive
5-5-8 Minamiaoyama
1F Nowhere Building
Minato-ku
Tokyo
bape.com

BBC/Ice Cream
4-28-22 Jingumae
Shibuya-ku
Tokyo
bbcicecream.com

Kinetics
4-31-2 Jingumae
Shibuya-ku
Tokyo
rakuten.ne.jp

F.I.L. by Visvim
B1 Floor 5-9-17 Jingumae
Shibuya-ku
Tokyo
visvim.tv

Neighborhood
4-32-7 Jingumae
Shibuya-ku
Tokyo
Japan
neighborhood.jp

Undefeated
4-28-2 Jingumae, 2nd floor
Shibuya-ku
Tokyo
undftd.com

Australia

Brisbane

Culture Kings
115 Queen Street Mall
Brisbane City, QLD 4000
Australia
culturekings.com.au

Urban Wear
262 Kingston Road, Slacks Creek
Brisbane City, QLD 4147
urbanwearonline.com.au

Melbourne

Someday
Level 3 Curtin House
252 Swanston Street
Melbourne, VIC 3000
someday-store.com

Up There Store
Level 1
15 McKillop St
Melbourne, VIC 3000
uptherestore.com

Spares
368 Smith St
Collingwood
Melbourne, VIC 3066
sparesstore.com.au

Sydney

Culture Kings
420 George Street
Sydney, NSW 2000
culturekings.com.au

ESPIONAGE
Shop 2
22–26 Goulburn Street,
Sydney, NSW 2000
sneakers4life.com

BONAFIDE
Shop 4
27–33 Goulburn Street
Sydney, NSW 2000
bnfde.com

New Zealand

Auckland

QUBIC STORE
154-160 Broadway Newmarket,
Auckland 1023
qubicstore.com

Area 51
55 High Street
Auckland 1010
area51store.co.nz

Christchurch

Infinite Definite Boutique
111 Cashel Street
Christchurch
infinitedefinite.com

Wellington

Good as Gold
120 Victoria Street
Wellington City 6011
goodasgold.co.nz

Acknowledgements

Thank you to my hearts Sarah Hernandez-Bedford, Jano and Jaida Bryden, Pat Allem, Sam Bryden. A big thank you to Ali Gitlow, Brad Farrant, Gimme 5 London and all the people at Goodhood. Thanks also to Norse Projects, A Number of Names, Yoon and Mai at Ambush, Carri Munden, Ollie Adegboye, Acyde, Tremaine, Tash Bleu and the CLOT Crew in Hong Kong. Thank you Gary Warnett, Charlie Morgan, Joe Swide at Ebbets Field, Aaron Sanders at Refuel Brands, Corey Kamenoff, Dan Jagger Ball, Otis, Rob, Seth Bradley, Tan Gillies at Nike and Samantha Fogden at New Era.

Front cover: ©Goodhood Studio. Opening image: ©Treu Bleu Imagery (p. 4). Introduction: ©Steven Bryden (p. 6). The Cap: A History: ©New Era (p. 8); ©Photography Collection, Miriam and Ira D. Wallach Division of Art, Prints and Photographs, The New York Public Library, Astor, Lenox and Tilden Foundations (p. 10). Anatomy of a Cap: ©George Simkin (pp. 12–13). Major Players: ©American Needle (p. 14); ©New Era (pp. 16–17); ©Starter (p. 18); ©Mitchell & Ness (pp. 20–21); ©American Needle (pp. 22–23); ©Ebbets Field Flannels (p. 24); ©Victor Osorio (p. 26); ©NBAE/Getty Images (p. 27). Cap Data: All ©Goodhood Studio (pp. 28–115). Influencers and Innovators: ©Jon Taguchi/Nike (p. 116); ©Treu Bleu Imagery (p. 118); ©F As In Frank (p. 120); ©Shawn Brackbill (p. 122); ©Ollie Adegboye (p. 124 and 126); ©Sarah De Burgh (p. 128); ©Ollie Adegboye (p. 130); ©Mia Haggi (p. 132); ©Toma Abuzz (p. 134); ©Ollie Adegboye (p. 136); ©Jon Taguchi/Nike (p. 138); ©Victor Osorio (p. 140). Caps Made Famous: ©NBC Universal/Getty Images (p. 142); ©Transcendental Graphics/Hulton Archive/Getty Images (p. 144); ©National Baseball Hall of Fame Library/MLB/Getty Images (p. 145 left); ©Transcendental Graphics/Archive Photos/Getty Images (p. 145 right); ©Mark Kauffman/Time & Life Pictures/Getty Images (p. 146); ©Joseph Scherschel/Time & Life Pictures/Getty Images (p. 147); ©Rich Pilling/Hulton Archive/Getty Images (p. 148 left); ©Photo File/Hulton Archive/Getty Images (p. 148 right); ©Roger Viollet/Getty Images (p. 149); ©L. Cohen/Wire Image/Getty Images (p. 150); ©NBC Universal/Getty Images (p. 151); ©Steve Eason/Hulton Archive/Getty Images (p. 152); ©Sports Illustrated Classic/Getty Images (p. 153); ©Juan Riviera/Roulette Fine Art/Getty Images (p. 154); ©Catherine McGann/Hulton Archive/Getty Images (p. 155); ©Ronald Grant Archive/Universal Pictures/Amblin Entertainment (p. 156); ©Ronald Grant Archive/Columbia/Tristar Pictures (p. 157 top left); ©Ronald Grant Archive/Lucasfilm (p. 157 bottom left); ©Paramount/The Kobal Collection/Phillip Caruso (p. 157 right); ©Paramount/The Kobal Collection (p. 158); ©Ronald Grant Archive/Longview Entertainment/Universal Pictures (p. 159 top left); ©Morgan Creek/Warner Bros/The Kobal Collection/Redin, Van (p. 159 bottom left); ©Bureau L.A. Collection/Sygma/Corbis (p. 159 top right); ©Ronald Grant Archive/Mandalay Entertainment (p. 159 bottom right); ©Time & Life/Getty Images (p. 160); ©Bob Thomas/Bob Thomas Sports Photography/Getty Images (p. 161 left); ©Richard Mackson/Sports Illustrated/Getty Images (p. 161 right); ©Jennifer Young/AFP/Getty Images (p. 162); ©Time & Life Pictures/Getty Images (p. 163); ©Chris Lopez/Sony Music Archive/Getty Images (p. 164); ©Ron Galella/WireImage/Getty Images (p. 165 left); ©Alexandra Wyman/WireImage/Getty Images (p. 165 right); ©John Parra/WireImage/Getty Images (p. 166 left); ©Tim Mosenfelder/Getty Images Entertainment/Getty Images (p. 166 right); ©Timothy A. Clary/AFP/Getty Images (p. 167); ©Mark Thompson/Getty Images Sport/Getty Images (p. 168); ©Clive Rose/Getty Images Sport/Getty Images (p. 169); ©Kevin Winter/Getty Images Entertainment/Getty Images (p. 170 left); ©Alan Chapman/Stringer/2012 FilmMagic (p. 170 right); ©Will Robson-Scott (p. 171). Street Snaps: ©Treu Bleu Imagery (pp. 172, 174–175); ©Megan McIssac (pp. 176–177); ©Ollie Adegboye (pp. 178–179); ©Toma Abuzz (pp. 180–181); ©Elsa Quarsell (pp. 182–183); ©Irwin Wong (pp. 184–185); ©Dan Hillman (pp. 186–187). Back cover: ©Goodhood Studio.

FSC
www.fsc.org
MIX
Paper from
responsible sources
FSC® C020353

Prestel Verlag, Munich
A member of Verlagsgruppe Random House GmbH

Prestel Verlag Neumarkter Strasse 28, 81673 Munich
Tel. +49 (0)89 4136-0 / Fax +49 (0)89 4136-2335
www.prestel.de

Prestel Publishing Ltd. 14–17 Wells Street, London W1T 3PD
Tel. +44 (0)20 7323 5004 / Fax +44 (0)20 7323 0271

Prestel Publishing 900 Broadway, Suite 603, New York, NY 10003
Tel. +1 (212) 995-2720 / Fax +1 (212) 995-2733
www.prestel.com

Library of Congress Control Number: 2013938776

British Library Cataloguing-in-Publication Data: a catalogue record for this book is available from the British Library; Deutsche Nationalbibliothek holds a record of this publication in the Deutsche Nationalbibliografie; detailed bibliographical data can be found under: http://dnb.d-nb.de

Prestel books are available worldwide. Please contact your nearest bookseller or one of the above addresses for information concerning your local distributor.

Editorial direction: Ali Gitlow
Editor: Eve Dawoud
Copyediting: Martha Jay
Design and layout: Goodhood Studio
Production: Friederike Schirge
Origination: Reproline Mediateam, Munich
Printing and binding: Neografia a.s.
Printed in Slovakia
Verlagsgruppe Random House FSC®-DEU-0100
The FSC®-certified paper Profimatt has been supplied by Igepa, Germany
ISBN 978-3-7913-4852-3